AMERICA
GOES
TO
THE
FAIR

Some Other Books by Lila Perl

ETHIOPIA,
Land of the Lion

EAST AFRICA,
Kenya, Tanzania, Uganda

Lila Perl

AMERICA GOES TO THE FAIR

All
About
State
and
County
Fairs
in
the
USA

illustrated with 64 photographs

William Morrow and Company
New York   1974

Library of Congress Cataloging in Publication Data

Perl, Lila.
  America goes to the fair.

  1. Agricultural exhibitions—United States—Juvenile literature.
2. United States—Fairs—Juvenile literature. I. Title.
S555.P47   917.3′03′074   74-5938
ISBN 0-688-21830-X
ISBN 0-688-31830-4 (lib. bdg.)

All photographs are by Lila Perl with the exception of the following: New York Public Library Picture Collection, pages 21, 24, 25, 26, 28, 30, 31, 32, 34, 36, 38, 40, 41, 44, 88, 103, 105; Nowak/Voss Advertising and Public Relations, pages 56, 58, 68 bottom, 84, 94 bottom, 97 top, 98 bottom, 113, 114, 115; New York State Fair, pages 61, 67, 68 top, 69, 70, 80, 82 top and bottom, 109, 112; Southeastern Fair, Atlanta, Georgia, frontispiece, pages 64, 94 top, 97 bottom, 110, 111. Permission is gratefully acknowledged.

This book is dedicated to
Esther Twentyman,
Director, Art and Home Center,
New York State Fair,
whose warmth, vision, and invaluable aid
made its writing possible.

The author also wishes to thank Mr. Bernard W. Potter, Director, New York State Fair; Mrs. Helen Vandervort, former Director of the Art and Home Center; Helen Burzynski of the Art and Home Center; Mrs. Eleanor M. Peavey, 4-H Cooperative Extension Agent, Onondaga County, New York; Mr. Maurice C. Coleman, General Manager, and Mrs. Martha Moon, Administrative Assistant, Southeastern Fair, Atlanta, Georgia.

Contents

AMERICA
GOES
TO
THE
FAIR

A
Word
About
Fairs

The blare of the midway, a ride on the monorail, a perfectly matched pair of prize-winning oxen, a tumbling cornucopia of pumpkin-gold harvest fruits, grandstand thrills at the demolition derby. . . . All of these experiences have been encountered, at one time or another, by fair visitors in the U.S.A.

Fairs in America come in all sizes. There are small country fairs held for one day only, in some generous farmer's grassy meadow. There are large state fairs that last a week or more and bring families in campers and trailers from hundreds of miles away. And there are enormous expositions, often called world's fairs, that last for months and bring exhibitors and visitors from halfway around the world.

Whatever their size or scope, their duration or purpose, fairs are for people. They tell people about other people, about the way they live and work, about their efforts to improve the quality of their lives and the lives of others—and about their triumphs when they succeed.

A fair may tell us something about the life of people on the next farm, ten miles down the road, or about the work of scientists in a laboratory or on a spaceship.

In their oldest and simplest form, fairs were a means of

bringing people together to trade, by bartering or by buying and selling. Market fairs, as they were called, served mankind from the very beginnings of civilization. Commerce and communication sprang from the primitive fairs of prehistory.

In their more advanced form, fairs became display cases and competitive exhibitions, places for setting high standards and offering examples to others. The subject might be farm products, household crafts, or the marvelous inventions and developments of the industrial revolution and the space age. But the object was always betterment. The United States, as a young republic just after the Revolutionary War, had a great deal to do with the transformation of the traditional market fair into the show-and-competition fair.

Today, as the United States rounds out its first 200 years as an independent nation, many people begin to wonder why we still need fairs. All fairs, they argue, have become too commercial. State and county fairs, in particular, are often dusty and dirty, hot and noisy, irritating and numbing. And most of all fairs are terribly, terribly tiring. In an era of supermarkets and department stores, movies and television, we ourselves may wonder why people still go to fairs.

The special magic of fairs is that they tell us, in a very firsthand way, about both ourselves and the world around us. Young people learn and develop through direct experience at fairs. The submission of a 4-H club project on the raising of broiler chicks or the examination of a human-blood chemistry study in a state fair's Hall of Science can each have a vital impact on youth.

One teaches techniques, possibly leading to a career as a poultry farmer. Or perhaps it merely provides the satisfaction of a job well done and the pleasure of explaining the birth of baby chicks to visitors at the 4-H exhibit in the Youth

Hall. The other may ignite only a fleeting interest in a young person's mind. Or it may spark a curiosity and concern that will lead to a profession in medicine or biochemistry.

Many people, however, overlook the educational and inspirational values of fairs and think of them mainly as a means of pleasant diversion. They are that, too. A farm boy may tell you that he has come to the fair simply to enter a pet rabbit, hoping to win a blue ribbon for excellence; a teen-ager may attend for the participatory thrill of riding the Twister or winning a stuffed animal for his admiring girl friend at a game of skill or chance; a family may be seeking the pleasures of a day's outing, with suitable diversions for all of its members; a senior citizen may want a look at the glistening rows of homemade jellies and the winning patchwork quilt in the Home Center exhibition.

The basic philosophy of fairs—local, state, or international—is to offer "something for everyone." Equally important for the survival of fairs is that they must adapt to change. If fairs in the United States have become larger, louder, more hucksterlike, that too, for better or for worse, is a sign of the changing times.

In any event, we can safely say that fairs are a reflection of the occupations and interests, achievements and aspirations of mankind.

I

FAIRS
PAST

1

How
Fairs
Began

Nobody knows when the very first fair was held, or where. Possibly it took place when two Stone Age men met beside a stream, near the cave dwellings of prehistoric Europe, Asia, or Africa, and decided to trade a diamond-hard flint for a warm, shaggy animal pelt, or a stone-bladed axe for a harpoonlike fishing spear.

Meetings for the purpose of barter are surely as old as mankind, but we can be quite certain that these prehistoric "fairs" were held by accident. After a time, groups of people or entire tribes probably did meet by prearrangement so that each could exchange items that were plentiful among them for those that were scarcer. But the idea of fairs held at regular intervals was still a long way off.

With the dawn of agriculture (about 6000 B.C.) and the growth of settled farming communities, people began to specialize in carpentry and weaving, in pottery and metalworking, as well as in the kinds of crops they grew and the kinds of livestock they raised. The harvest period became the ideal time for meeting, exhibiting, and trading both agricultural products and handcrafted wares. So the time for holding market fairs, in these societies, became more or less established. Of course, all such fairs were local ones, for means of transportation were extremely limited, even though man had arrived by now in the New Stone Age.

Around 3000 B.C. the manual skills that man had developed, as a result of having a dependable food supply, began to contribute to the growth of great civilizations in certain parts of the world. Mesopotamia, in the then-fertile valley of the Tigris and Euphrates rivers or what is today Iraq, was one; ancient Egypt, bordering the well-irrigated banks of the Nile, was another. Fairs grew in number and size along with these civilizations.

By 2000 B.C. a people called the Phoenicians occupied the rich land of cedar groves that lay between the Lebanese Mountains and the Mediterranean Sea, today known as Lebanon. The Bible gives us our first report of the magnificient Middle Eastern fairs that were held in the Phoenician coastal city of Tyre, which flourished for over a thousand years.

In Ezekiel 27:12-24, we learn of the silver, iron, tin, and lead from Asia Minor (now Turkey), the precious stones and rich embroideries from Syria, the horses from Arabia, the ivory and slaves from Africa, the spices, gold, wheat, honey, oil, wine, and fine white wool that came by caravan to the Phoenician coast from India, Persia, and other distant reaches of Asia.

Among the attractions of Tyre as a fair center were the unusual wares that the Phoenicians themselves manufactured and offered in trade. Glass, a rarity in the ancient world, and marvelously wrought metal jewelry encrusted with precious stones were products of their special skills. But perhaps most sought after was the rich purple-dyed woolen and linen cloth that the Phoenicians alone produced. A color such as Phoenician purple had never been seen before, and fabrics of this hue were so rare, so in demand, and so costly that purple soon

Phoenician sea merchants introducing their wares
at a distant fairground

became established, almost the world over, as the color of
royalty.

There were other great fair centers in the Near East, such
as the city of Mecca in Arabia and Damascus in Syria. But the
Phoenicians' great advantage was that they were bold and fear-
less sea traders as well as land traders. They cut the cedars of
their native land and fashioned them into sturdy, crescent-
prowed sailing vessels. By 1200 B.C. they were sending ships to
Spain at the western end of the Mediterranean Sea and even
up the Atlantic coast of Europe as far north as Cornwall in
southwest England.

Using the seas and oceans, the Phoenicians opened new highways to the fairgrounds of the world and became the great

seagoing salesmen of their day. The attraction of their own markets at home was enhanced by the raw copper and tin that these expert metalworkers brought back with them from Europe. Of great importance, too, was salt, that precious food preservative of ancient times—evaporated from the coastal marshes of Spain—which the Phoenicians obtained for their glass, jewelry, purple cloth, and other manufactured wares.

With the rise of great European civilizations, fair centers moved west. The first regularly held, large fairs of Europe probably developed around the Greek games that took place at fixed intervals at Olympia, Delphi, and other sites in ancient Greece. The games were not only athletic contests featuring running events, boxing, chariot racing, and the like, they were religious festivals in honor of gods or goddesses, each worshipped in his or her own sanctuary. The Olympic games, in honor of Zeus, were held every four years in summer and are believed to have begun as early as 776 B.C.

Huge crowds gathered on these occasions and along with them came traders, merchants, and vendors of all sorts to serve the immediate needs of the people with food, drink, sandals, and warm blankets. But the games offered an even greater advantage for those with goods to sell or trade, for during the time they were being held hostilities ceased, soldiers patrolled the roads, and crimes were promptly and severely punished. As a result, valuable objects such as spices, cloth, carpets, glassware, and armor were also brought to the Greek fairs, protected by the sanctity of the holy event.

The priests of ancient Greece did not object. It was under their authority that the traders were permitted to display and sell their merchandise, and the priests became involved in money changing and money lending, often to their own financial advantage.

The Romans continued the practice of holding fairs in connection with religious festivals, and it is no accident that the very word, *fair,* comes from the Latin *feriae* meaning "holidays." The Italian *fiera,* the Spanish *feria,* and the French *foire*—all meaning fair—are also derived from the Latin. Rome's most important religious festival and accompanying public fair was held in honor of Jupiter, chief god of ancient Rome and the counterpart of Zeus in ancient Greece. The celebration took place every year in April and was, in fact, called the Feria Latina, or Latin Fair. Fairs were also held on the feast days of other Roman gods and goddesses, particularly those that presided over trade, harvests, the hunt, and music and poetry. Elections and other political events in ancient Rome were additional occasions when major fairs took place.

Of course, Rome had its ordinary market fairs too. They were held every ninth day and were, therefore, called *nundinae* (from *novem dies,* or "nine day"). On these occasions, country folk came into the city with farm produce and livestock to trade for manufactured articles or for products imported to Rome from its territories abroad. The government used the *nundinae* as a time and place for publicly announcing any new laws or decrees to the populace.

With their genius for roadbuilding and lawgiving, the Romans did much to facilitate the growth of fairs and to set the rules for how they should be conducted, protecting both buyers and sellers from harm and from dishonest practices. Rome's influence was strong in Gaul and in Britain, as well as in the other far-flung conquered lands of the Empire. Although Rome fell in the fifth century A.D., northern European fairs from medieval times right up to the present show patterns based on the fairs of ancient Rome.

An Italian religious fair, in the Greek and Roman tradition,
held in honor of Saint Luke

   With the birth of the Christian Era, fairs had begun to be
held in honor of Christian saints instead of the gods of ancient
civilizations. During the early Middle Ages, in 629, a Frankish
king, Dagobert I, decreed the Fair of Saint Denis in France.
The fair was administered under a royal charter by the monks
of the Abbey of Saint Denis near Paris, and, as in ancient
Greece and Rome, the religious authorities offered protection
to traders from thievery and more serious crimes. The monks
saw nothing wrong with running a commercial enterprise, for
many people who came to trade near the church might also
be attracted to worship.
   Charlemagne, the greatest of the Frankish kings, promoted
fairs on both sides of the Rhine in the late 700's, for he believed strongly in the value of commerce. As the church was

A Frankish bishop blessing the seventh-century Fair of Saint Denis #2

deeply involved with fair operations in Germany as well as in France, the German word for *fair* became *Messe,* meaning "mass," and the word in the Low Countries of Belgium and Holland became *kirmess* (church mass) or kermis.

Throughout the greater part of the Middle Ages, however, commerce came almost to a standstill in Europe. People lived and worked on feudal estates, providing almost all of their own needs—food, clothing, farming implements, rude home furnishings, and the like. Salt, for the preservation of meat and other foods, was one of the few necessities that was not generally available on the feudal estates of France and Germany, and often local fairs grew up around this trade alone.

With the decline of feudalism, beginning in the twelfth century, trade and commerce on a larger and more interna-

A Chinese fair of Marco Polo's time

tional scale began to flower in Europe. The Crusades to the
Holy Land, starting in 1095 and continuing for over two
centuries, brought Europeans in contact with the Near East,
with its spices, rich gold- and silver-threaded cloths, intricate
metalwork and leatherwork. Marco Polo's visit to China in
the 1200's brought new products, ranging from silks to gun-
powder, to Europe. In addition, the famed Venetian explorer
told of the great fair at Kinsai, in the Chinese empire of the
Mongol ruler, Kublai Khan.

He reported that at Kinsai there were ten huge squares,
each with its own palace of justice to settle trade arguments.
The fair was held every third day and played host to hundreds
of thousands of people from all over China. Europeans found
it difficult to imagine a fair on such a large scale. Of the vari-

ety of foods and manufactured wares traded at Kinsai, probably the most important item was pepper, which was prized
as was salt in Europe. It was said that over five tons of pepper were sold each trading day.

These Eastern influences, plus the increased wealth of the
kings, dukes, counts, and other nobles who had once been
feudal lords but had won out over their fellows, stimulated
European fairs to grow larger and more international after
the 1200's. Outstanding were the fairs held in the regions of
Champagne and Brie in northeastern France, those in the
cities of Leipzig and Nuremberg in Germany, and Antwerp
and Bruges in Belgium. The counts of Champagne, like other
powerful new rulers of the late Middle Ages, took a personal
hand in the running of the fairs, setting up an equable system
of taxes and tariffs. The international standard of troy weight
was developed at the fairs held in the town of Troyes, the
capital of the Champagne region. Now at last coins, metals
such as gold and silver, and many kinds of jewels could be
measured to determine their value based on a twelve-ounce
pound.

This system made the use of money at fairs and markets
much more practical. Even though the coins brought by traders
from both near and distant places came in a bewildering array
of sizes, weights, and metals, there was now a way of assess-
ing their worth against the item to be purchased, and the
clumsier system of barter could be done away with in many
cases. French and German fairs in the thirteenth century also
added exciting new entertainment features such as fire eating
and tightrope dancing in order to attract the public in greater
numbers.

The greatest international fair of the Middle Ages—the
one that could truly be said to link East and West—was the

The great international fair at Nizhni Novgorod in Russia

huge fair at Nizhni Novgorod in Russia. Believed to have started around 1366, the fair was regularly held for nearly six centuries until it was finally abolished by the government of the Soviet Union in 1930 because it was disruptive of the new socialist economic system.

As land travel was so difficult before the era of railroads and motor highways, the site chosen for the fair was on the Volga River at a point where another major river, the Oka, joined it. Barges and other types of transport vessels could unload their cargoes almost directly onto the level river plain where the fair was held. The name of the town itself, Nizhni Novgorod, meaning "lower new city," was changed in 1932, and it may be found on maps today under its new name: Gorki.

The Volga, Europe's longest river, brought wares to the Nizhni Novgorod fair from northern Europe via the Baltic Sea, from Persia and India via the Caspian Sea, and from China over one of the most difficult land-and-water routes in the world. The main item of trade from China was tea. The extent of tea drinking in Russia grew by means of the Nizhni Novgorod fair, which also influenced the British and other Western peoples to become tea drinkers.

Over the centuries, systems of canals improved the water routes leading to Nizhni Novgorod. By the 1800's the fair was at the peak of its development, a world bazaar of unmatched variety and scope. Millinery from Paris and furs from Siberia, English woolens and Tartar horse pelts, caviar and dried fish, boots and all sorts of leather goods, armor and weapons, Bohemian crystal, raw silk, and ornate furniture were only a few of the kinds of goods offered for sale or barter during the six weeks in August and September that the fair ran.

Merchants were assigned booths or stalls laid out in orderly rows. The fair was run by a committee under the authority of the provincial governor. As in the typical Eastern *souk* or Oriental bazaar, shops selling a particular kind of merchandise, whether gold jewelry or ironware, holy icons or Persian carpets, were all restricted to a given area so that customers could compare prices and competition would be encouraged.

The fair had its squalid side, too. It was frequented by beggars with dreadful sores and mutilations, the sanitary arrangements were crude, and a dust-filled, odorous heat often settled over the river plain in late summer. Men were said to outnumber women at the fair by one hundred to one. A smaller winter fair was usually also held at Nizhni Novgorod. At that time of year it was set up on the ice of the frozen Oka River. The last of the winter fairs took place in 1864, when an unexpected January thaw melted the river's surface, dashing fair booths and livestock, horses and men, into the frigid waters.

In Britain, following the end of Roman rule, fairs and markets sprang up with the influx of the Germanic-speaking peoples, the Angles, Saxons, and Jutes, who began arriving in the fifth century. The greatest of the English fairs, and the one that most influenced those British subjects who later became American colonists, was the renowned Stourbridge Fair held at Cambridge in eastern England.

The charter for the fair is believed to have been granted by King John in 1211 as a means of benefiting a church-hospital for lepers. But Cambridge was also a key location for commerce because of its bridge that spanned the Cam River and permitted trade between eastern and central England. In addition, goods could be shipped directly to the fair by way of the river. Later in the thirteenth century, the first college of

An English "frost fair" held on the frozen Thames, patterned on the winters fairs of Russia

Bargaining at a pig fair in rural Ireland

Cambridge University was established, but the fair came first. The fair itself took its name from the nearby Stour River.

The most important items of trade at the Stourbridge Fair were woolens and other woven goods for clothing, draperies, upholstery, blankets, quilts, and the like, and hops for the brewing of beer. Clothiers, tailors, and wool merchants sold their articles in the large central square of the fairground known as the Duddery. The name of the square came from the Middle English word *dudde,* which we still use today when we say "duds," meaning "clothes." By the beginning of the fourteenth century, Stourbridge Fair was attracting foreign goods—Venetian glass and Flemish linens, French wines, Russian furs, and Baltic amber—as well as agricultural and manufactured products from all over the British Isles.

The rules of the fair were announced at each year's opening by a proclamation known as "crying the fair." Among the regulations "cried" in 1548 were notices to fairgoers to leave their weapons behind when entering the fairgrounds, and for men and women alike to maintain good behavior. Bakers were told to identify their loaves with a mark and advised what kinds and sizes of bread to bake and how much to charge for them; brewers and wine sellers were warned to give honest measures, as were herring and eel sellers; butchers and pike mongers were cautioned to sell only fresh and untainted meat and fish. Innkeepers and charcoal sellers, grain merchants and wool merchants also were given sets of rules by which to abide.

For those who disregarded the law, there was swift justice dealt out by the "pie powder" court, a judicial body that sat at each fair to deal specifically with crimes and misdemeanors arising on the fairgrounds. The name, *pie powder,* comes from the French *pied poudreux* meaning "dusty foot," and applied to the dusty-booted peddlers and other foot-traveling merchants who were found guilty of most of the petty swindling that took place.

By the latter half of the nineteenth century the Stourbridge Fair had diminished in importance, lasting only three days instead of three weeks as it had during its prime. Nevertheless, it established a pattern for the trade fairs of Colonial America.

Entertainment at an English fair,
similar to the great Stourbridge Fair

2

Early
American
Fairs

The first English and Dutch colonists in North America perched their settlements along the Eastern seaboard, facing toward Europe. At their backs lay a sprawling, unknown continent. It was only natural for the English to want to create a "new England," for the Dutch to want to create a "new Netherland," in the raw wilderness of the New World. Insofar as it was possible, they copied the clothing, housing, and eating patterns, manners, and customs of their European ancestors and relatives.

So it was not surprising that the first fairs to be held on American soil were market fairs in the European tradition. On Manhattan Island, in New Netherland, the Dutch governor decreed only a few years after its settlement in 1625 that there should be two regularly held annual fairs—a fair for the sale of cattle on October 15 and a fair for the sale of hogs on November 1. On Long Island, where a group of cattle farmers jointly purchased a bit of territory called Cow Neck (now the Manhasset-Port Washington area), the first cattle fair was held in 1641.

By the 1650's, the Dutch in New Amsterdam were running kermis fairs similar to those of their homeland. Although

33

An early American livestock fair

held under church auspices, the fairs of the fun-loving Dutch tended to be lively and even boisterous. In addition to trading, there was entertainment such as puppet shows, tightrope dancing, fortune-telling, and the well-loved buffoonery of some Merry Andrew, the traditional clown character of European fairs.

However, as professional entertainment acts were not always available, fairgoers also made their own fun by participating in competitions such as grinning contests or in whistling contests to see who could whistle a given tune most clearly and for the longest time without breaking up. Races were held for men, boys, and even women. Obstacle races and sack races, in which the contestant had to "run" with a bag tied around his legs, were popular. For young men, there were much rowdier contests, such as trying to catch a pig with a greased tail or "pulling the goose," which involved grabbing hold of a greased live goose. Prizes ranged from a plug of tobacco or a pot of pudding to a length of fine woven cloth or a purse of money.

Horse racing was a favorite event at Long Island fairs just as it was at those of the Southern colony of Virginia. Jamaica (now part of Queens County, New York City) was a fine, grassy meadowland, ideal for breeding horses. Like the South, Long Island had its large farming estates worked by staffs of black slaves brought from Africa.

Southern fairs were often gala social events held in cities like Williamsburg, Virginia, or Charleston, South Carolina, and attended by wealthy plantation owners with their wives and families. The daytime activities of horse and livestock trading, buying and selling land, and paying off debts would be crowned on the final evening with an elegant ball to which the ladies wore imported finery purchased in the cities that played host to the fair.

Early New England fairs were much more restrained than those of the South or the Middle Atlantic region. In Massachusetts and Connecticut especially, the Puritan influence was strong and merriments such as "idle games" were frowned upon. Business was the main purpose, beginning with New England's first cattle fair, held at New Haven in 1644.

New Englanders, in fact, were so intent on business that some shopkeepers objected to the fairs, which usually were scheduled from one to four times a year in the various localities, and to the weekly markets in the towns, on the ground that the middleman's profit was eliminated in direct buyer-seller transactions. Established shopkeepers also objected to the Yankee peddler, a traveling salesman who sometimes turned up at fairs but more often went door to door among

Flocking to a simple New England country fair

the scattered farm dwellings selling needles and combs, tin-ware and tableware, food staples and drugstore remedies. It was true that some peddlers were dishonest. Connecticut, the Nutmeg State, was originally called the Wooden Nutmeg State because peddlers traversing its territory were said to have sold "nutmegs" carved out of wood and soaked in nutmeg extract. These held up very poorly when the housewife attempted to grind some powdered spice for use in a pudding or a cake!

But local fairs and markets and traveling salesmen were necessary in the colonies, which were made up mainly of small, isolated farming communities. As the period of the American Revolution approached, over 95 percent of the Colonial population was living and working on the land. And the country that emerged from the Revolutionary War in 1783 was still overwhelmingly agricultural.

Being citizens of an independent nation gave the farmers of the young United States a fresh sense of purpose and a driving new ambition. As early as 1785, an agricultural society was formed in Philadelphia. True, its founders were mainly political figures who also happened to be gentlemen farmers rather than simple working farmers. But at least the idea of gathering and spreading information about what crops to grow, what livestock to raise, and how best to do so for profit and plenty in the new land came under consideration.

A New York agricultural society, organized in 1791, gave serious thought to such matters as manuring the land with seaweed, domesticating the elk and the moose for use as meat animals, harnessing the buffalo to work as a draft animal in the fields, growing poppy plants for opium, and making whisky out of potatoes. They also discussed less difficult projects—the feeding of hogs, the growing of corn, and how to prevent wheat smut and diseases of orchard trees.

A new day was dawning for American agriculture. It was no longer considered adequate to farm in the old Colonial way, sowing Indian crops such as corn, beans, and pumpkin, European wheat, rye, and garden vegetables, and raising English livestock. New materials and methods were called for, and there was the whole world to choose from. But the "dirt farmer" was not easily contacted or influenced by the learned men of the agricultural societies. There were not even any agricultural journals published at the time, and, if there had been, few would have read them, for many farmers were illiterate or semiliterate.

Then, in 1807, in Pittsfield, Massachusetts, a gentleman farmer by the name of Elkanah Watson decided that he would "show Americans how to farm" by providing some examples. Having just acquired a pair of Merino sheep imported from

Spain, Watson took the pure white, heavy-fleeced animals to the Pittsfield village green, where he tied them to an elm tree to exhibit them to his neighbors. To Watson's delight, a surprisingly large number of Berkshire County farmers and their wives turned out to examine the exotic, fine-wooled creatures.

Watson had been born in 1758 in Plymouth, Massachusetts, and had served General Washington in the early years of the Revolution. In 1779, he became a bearer of government dispatches to Benjamin Franklin in Paris. Between 1779 and 1784, he traveled widely in Europe, keeping alert to possibilities for the improvement of American agriculture and commerce.

Elkanah Watson, father of the American agricultural fair

Elkanah Watson was nearly fifty years old when he bought his farm at Pittsfield, but he was imbued with the desire somehow to help develop America's agricultural resources. In 1808, a year after showing his Merinos, Watson pointed out to his Massachusetts neighbors that the long-legged, large-boned hogs they were breeding were unprofitable, and he introduced them to a strain of fleshy, short-legged swine from Dutchess County, New York. Watson also showed Berkshire County farmers how to improve their cattle with a superior type of English breeding bull and how to dig ponds on their property and stock them with pickerel and other freshwater table fish.

The growing neighborhood interest in Watson's examples and exhibits relating to farm improvement encouraged him to plan a much larger event than his 1807 exhibit of two Merino sheep. It featured a music band, a parade, a float displaying an operating broadcloth loom and a working spinning jenny, and pens filled with a variety of prize-quality animals. One feature of the procession was a plow, drawn by sixty-nine chained oxen, upon which sat the oldest man in the county. Marchers wore badges of wheat in their hats as a reminder of the main theme: agriculture. This first-of-its-kind Berkshire County Fair was held on October 1, 1810.

In 1811, the Berkshire Agricultural Society was formed, with Elkanah Watson as president, and on September 24 of that year a second county fair was held. This time prizes totaling $70 were awarded for the best livestock, and over 3000 people attended.

In 1812, premium money was increased to $208, and Watson himself won a prize for a piece of fine wool broadcloth woven from the wool of his own sheep. He did not keep the prize money, however. For the fair of 1813, Watson enlisted the participation of women for the first time, offering prizes for cookery, needlework, and other household-arts products. That year the fair closed with an agricultural ball.

The American county fair had been born! Exhibition and competition were the twin functions instead of merely buying and selling, as at the old European-style market fairs. The American revolutionary spirit of "let's show 'em, boys" and "ever upward" had somehow been caught up and crystallized in the unique institution of the agricultural fair.

Competitive poultry exhibit at an agricultural fair

A social fling at a Vermont fair of the mid-1800's

In addition, Elkanah Watson had overcome the New Englander's reluctance to attend public events that dealt with other than religious or business matters. "Idle games" were not frowned upon when they took the form of a plowing match or a cattle competition for prize money. The county agricultural fair was clearly in the farmer's own interest, and he knew it. It was a means of education and an incentive toward a better life. If it also took care of the farmer's and his family's social and entertainment needs for a few days out of the working year, that too could be accepted as a beneficial aspect.

By 1820, agricultural societies, following the Berkshire example, had been formed all over New England, New York, and the South and were pointing as far west as the Mississippi Valley. And, in conjunction with the societies, county and local fairs were popping up in greater profusion every fall.

The first farm journals began to be published about this time and served to publicize both fairs and the work of the agricultural societies. The *Old Farmer's Almanack,* which had been providing farm families with news-and-information tidbits and simple home entertainment since 1792, offered its own tribute to the fast-growing institution with some lines in its calendar of October, 1824, just fourteen years after the first Berkshire County Fair was held.

> This is the month for cattle shows, and other agricultural exhibitions—Premiums are offered by various societies for the greatest crops; the best stock, and the best domestic manufactures, and thousands are pulling away for the prize, with all their might.
> The great bull of Farmer Lumpkins is a nosuch!
> Peter Nibble has raised a monstrous field of white beans!
> Jo Lucky's acre of corn has seven stout ears to the stalk!
> Dolly Dilligence has outstript all in the bonnet line!
> Tabitha Twistem's hearth rug is up to all Market-street!
> The Linsey-Woolsey Manufacturing Company have made the finest piece of satinet that ever mortals set eyes on!
> There is the widow Clacket's heifer, she is to be driven!
> And, O, if you could only see 'Squire Trulliber's great boar! They say it is as big as a full grown rhinoceros!
> Huzza, huzza for the premiums! Here's to the girl that can best darn a stocking, and to the lad that shall raise the biggest pumpkin!

After a slower period of growth during the 1820's and early 1830's, fairs came into the spotlight once again. Interest was spurred by a series of American inventions of marvelous new farm machines: Cyrus McCormick's reaper, demonstrated in 1831 and patented in 1834, John Deere's steel plow, developed in 1837, as well as new cultivators, planters, and threshers. What better way to exhibit the new machines to farmers and what better way for farmers to examine these fabulous agricultural aids than at their county and local fairs?

Meanwhile, as state governments became larger and more prosperous, they began to take an interest in agricultural matters on a statewide basis. In September of 1841, the year before Elkanah Watson's death, the nation's very first state fair was held at the village of Syracuse in the state of New York. Shortly afterward, New Jersey held its first state fair at New Brunswick. Michigan, Pennsylvania, Ohio, Wisconsin, Indiana, Illinois, and Iowa followed in the years between 1849 and 1854.

Today state fairs are held in nearly every state in the union along with several regional fairs in which a number of states participate. Together with county and local fairs, American fairgoers are given a choice of over 3200 fairs every year, reaching across the nation from Maine to Alaska.

Faced with this many fairs, most of them compressed into a six- to eight-week, late-summer and early-autumn period each year, it would be almost impossible for any one person to cover all of them within a human lifetime, even if anyone wanted to. In fact, attending a single fair can be a bewildering experience. Upon going through the entrance gate, the fair visitor often feels pulled in three hundred directions at once. The dizzying sky ride on the midway beckons crazily, a pair of doe-eyed oxen almost beg to be followed to the cattle barns, there is the screech and thunder of hell drivers whirling around the racetrack, the model New England village sits serenely across the shimmering waters of the swan pond, the odor of hamburgers and hot dogs, Italian peppers, Polish sausage, and Dutch waffles temptingly assaults the nostrils.

Although fairs are too inviting and too exciting to be very systematically explored on-the-scene, a good way to find out what makes fairs tick is to break them down into their major components: agricultural events; arts, crafts, and homemaking; youth and vocational activities; midway and entertainment events; and special exhibits.

So, along with the rest of America, let's go to the fair!

Poster commemorating 100 years of community settlement, but glorifying brutal Indian conquest.

II

FAIRS
PRESENT

3

Agricultural
Events

White-faced Herefords and coal-black Angus, speckled Holsteins and reddish-brown Jerseys, Suffolk sheep, Poland China hogs, and Toggenburg goats. . . . Most of these names for pure breeds of beef and dairy cattle and other important livestock mean little to anyone outside the approximately 3 percent of the American population who are today directly engaged in agriculture.

Back in 1807, when Elkanah Watson exhibited his famed pair of Merino sheep, about 93 percent of the American people were farmers, and they soon realized that it was important and helpful to them to know that Guernsey cattle produced milk that was particularly high in butterfat and that Duroc hogs gave birth to especially large litters of piglets.

Nowadays, however, well over 90 percent of the nation's 210 million people never know a real honest-to-goodness farm. So we may well wonder why the oldest state fair in the country, the New York State Fair, offers $65,000 in prize money for top-class cattle, sheep, swine, and dairy goats. Another $12,500 in state money goes to winners among poultry, pigeon, and rabbit entries. And additional large sums of special prize money are awarded in all of these categories by independent livestock-breeders' associations, poultry clubs, and the like.

At first it may appear that New York, and most other modern state and county fairs, are paying undue attention to agriculture. It is true that even farm families, which have become increasingly prosperous over the years, also come to fairs nowadays to view the newest comfort-and-convenience appliances, such as washer-dryers and microwave ovens, and family recreation vehicles like campers and snowmobiles. And it is also true that commercial exhibitors of everything from tulip bulbs to tombstones and from hula skirts to play-by-number home organs take up more and more room at the agricultural fair (and provide a good source of space-rental revenue to the fair treasury). But the important difference between a state or county fair and an amusement park or a shopping center is that it does feature agricultural as well as home and community services.

Those who would do away with the cattle judging and dairy-product displays, sheep-shearing contests and prize fruit-and-vegetable exhibits are forgetting that, while only 3 percent of Americans may be agricultural producers, all Americans are agricultural consumers. As the exploding world population threatens to outstrip the earth's food supply, all people have become more interested in learning about the sources of food production, as well as other naturally produced materials such as cotton and wool for our clothing, and wood and vegetable fibers for our homes.

On the level of firsthand experience, where but at an agricultural fair can the city or town dweller see so much of the science and practice of agriculture in a single day's visit? At the fair, the farming and the nonfarming population meet, and nonfarmers learn in both a general and a specific way.

For example, the New York City resident who makes a trip to his state fair at Syracuse will come away with an increased respect for the state's dairy industry. Over $29,000 in state prize money is awarded for dairy cattle alone, while the fair's modern Milk Quarter demonstrates the complete chain of milk processing from cow to carton.

A glass-encased New York State butter queen and her attendant, sculpted out of pure dairy butter

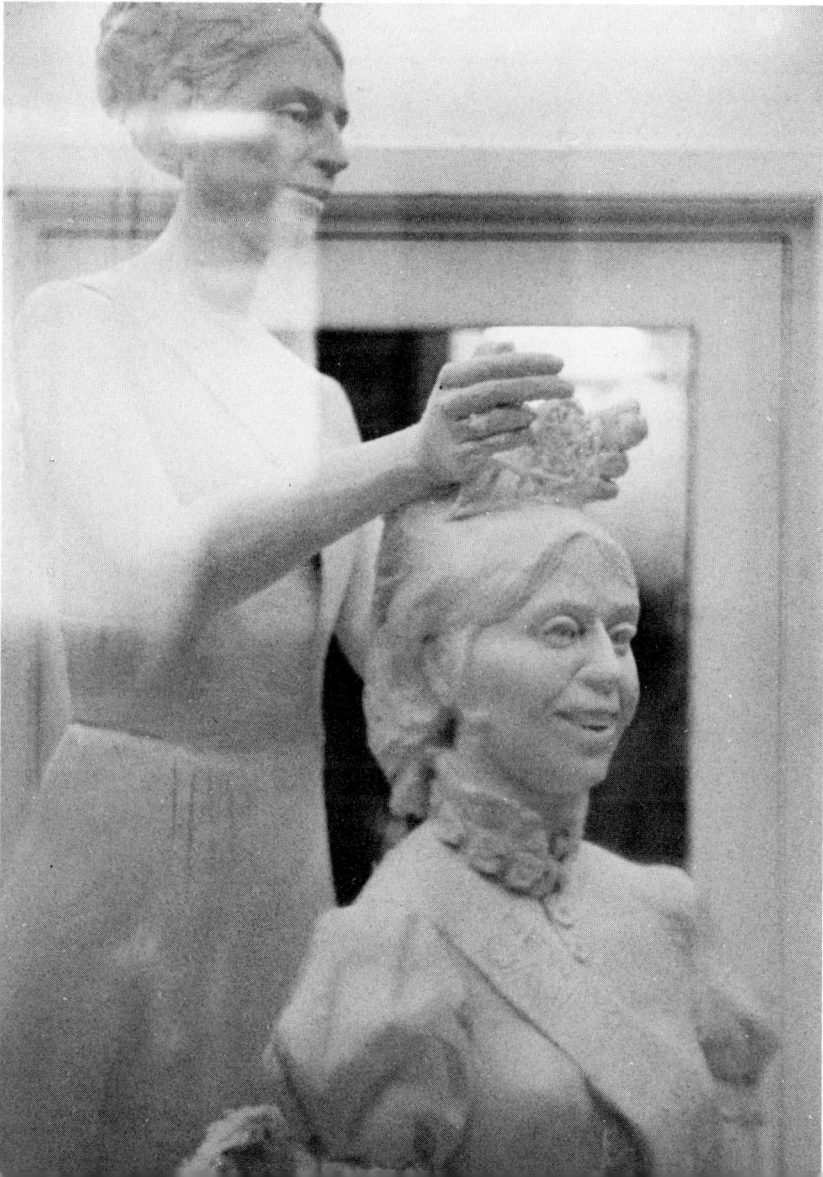

The big-city visitor will also be reminded that pure maple sugar, maple syrup, and maple cream are regional and richly historic New York State specialties. He will discover that few things taste better than a baked New York State potato slathered with a melting lump of golden New York State butter, both given away free in the Horticulture Building. And a visit to the goat barns at the edge of the fairground will convince him that his complimentary cup of frosty-cold goat's milk is rightfully billed as "udder joy!"

While acting as an informational and educational exhibit for the visitor, the fair serves as a vital showcase for the agricultural producer. From the farmer's point of view, what better place to promote the industry of the 3 percent who produce the food to the 100 percent who consume it? At the same time, the fair is a teaching ground where farmers, both young and old, can learn from other farmers. It is also an information center where experts can offer demonstrations of

Waiting for the cattle judging to begin
at a small country fair in Connecticut

services from soil analysis to a live performance of veterinary surgery. So, in spite of the shift from country to city living in the United States, agricultural events have continued to be an important aspect of fairs.

Livestock judging, one of the quietest and gentlest of fair activities, goes on today just as in the fairs of over 150 years ago. Usually the judges are farmers, cattle breeders, county officials, agricultural extension-service agents, or experts from the animal husbandry departments of agricultural colleges. The animals are divided into classes by breed, age, and sex, and they are judged for their contour, firmness of body flesh, distribution of weight, characteristic appearance, and suitability to function.

After observing the slowly paraded animals in a given contest and examining each carefully, the judge announces his decisions to their exhibitors and all onlookers, explaining that he has awarded first prize to a particular Angus bull because

Hampshire sheep line up for the final prize decision at a New England fair

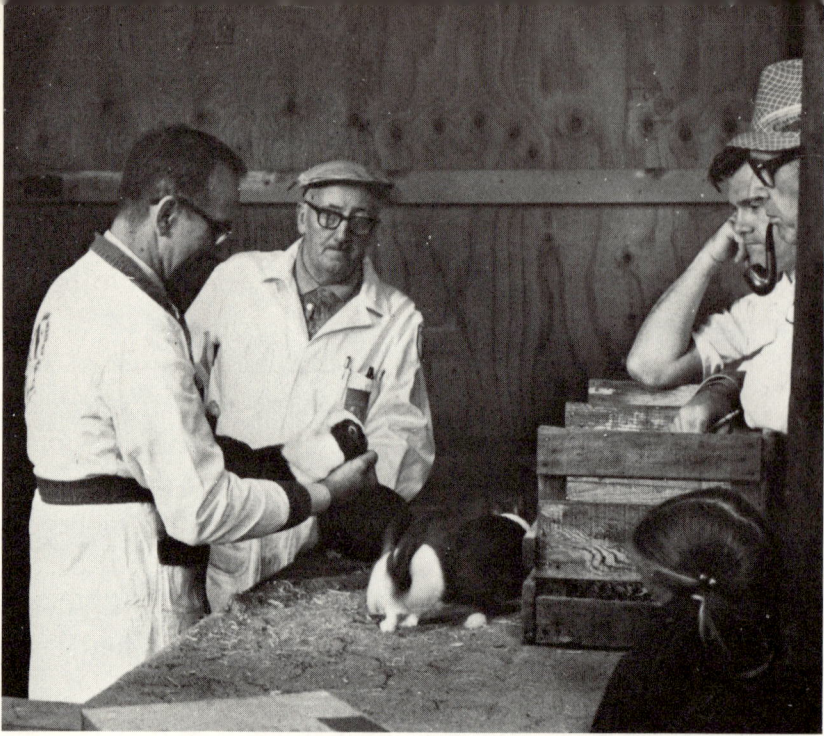

The serious business of evaluating a rabbit's best points

of his "strong loins and clean neck," or to a Holstein heifer for her "rump spread, neat rib and shoulder flesh, and the placement of her milking equipment."

Agricultural events that provide more activity and promote more general interest are contests such as the ox draw or ox pull. Some fairs feature pony pulls and draft-horse pulls as well. The ox pull is designed to test the strength of those docile, heavy-bodied animals that once plowed the fields of pioneer America and pulled the wagons westward. The event usually takes place on a grassy meadow or on the infield of the grandstand racetrack.

Each competing pair of oxen is hitched, in turn, to a metal sled onto which a number of cement blocks, ranging from a hundred to a thousand pounds in weight, have been power lifted. The yoked team is encouraged, urged, or threatened by its owner into bravely pulling the load forward for a distance that is then recorded by the judges. It is not unusual for a winning team to pull 6900 pounds six feet. After each pull, the sled is returned to its starting point by a winch harnessed to a farm tractor.

Tractors themselves compete at the agricultural fair. Just as the nineteenth-century farmer prided himself on the pulling power he could coax from his horse, ox, or mule team, the motorized farmer of the twentieth century sets great store by his all-purpose farm machine and by his skill in operating it.

Above: Coaxing a stalwart team of oxen
for a win in the traditional ox-pull event
Below: Getting ready for a tractor pull
on the New York State Fair's racetrack infield

Farm tractors, which first came into use in the United States around the turn of the century, today are manufactured in all sizes and shapes and are able to push or pull or power other farm machines including plows, planters, combines, hay balers, potato diggers, orchard sprayers, and many more. The tractor-pull event at fairs is similar to the ox pull, but of course the weights pulled are much greater, often into the 16,000-pound class.

Farm-machinery displays are the most important agricultural exhibits for most farmers as they could not otherwise view so many large and bulky pieces of equipment gathered together in one place. The Minnesota State Fair, located on a 300-acre fairground between Minneapolis and Saint Paul, boasts that its buildings and grounds on famed Machinery Hill display and demonstrate more tractors, grain elevators, feed-mills, and other latest models of farming equipment than at any other fair.

A keen interest in farm machinery, starting at an early age

While most people enjoy the colorful prize fruit-and-vegetable displays at fairs, admiring the shiniest purple eggplant, the largest muskmelon, and the tallest stalk of corn, few realize that competitions are also held for the best hay, cut and cured from alfalfa, clover, and other grasses, for the best silage, corn, grains, beans, sunflowers, and other farm-animal feeds. Silage, the nutritious summer feed stored for winter use in the tall, airtight farm silo, and other forage materials are usually judged off in a corner of the vast farm machinery building. Although not impressive to the eye of the casual viewer, they play a vital role in nourishing the dairy and meat animals on which American consumers so largely depend.

Flowers, exhibited both as individual blooms and in a variety of artistic arrangements, are judged in the horticultural competitions. Entries are submitted by farm people, suburbanites, garden clubs, and all sorts of enthusiastic home gardeners. Ornamental gourds, dried corn, dried flowers and grasses, and even evergreens grown for Christmas-tree use compete for prizes at state and county fairs.

A number of farmers' organizations have grown up in the United States since the early days of the agricultural societies of the post-Revolutionary era, and many of them are closely involved with agricultural and other activities at fairs. One outstanding body is the Grange, which operates on national, state, and local levels as a fraternal order devoted to education, recreation, and service for farm families.

The Grange was founded in 1867 by a government agricultural worker, Oliver Hudson Kelley, after he had toured the post-Civil War South for the Federal Department of Agriculture (which had been formed in 1862). Kelley observed

Prize, single-bloom flower exhibit at the New York State Fair

the poverty, ignorance, and low morale among farmers in the war-torn South and felt that a fraternal organization with social and educational goals would help to heal the national rift and improve Southern farming. The Grange later took on a political role also. Although it dropped much of its political initiative after the 1880's, it still plays a part in evaluating and supporting farm legislation today.

The Grange symbol is a seven-sided emblem with a sheaf of wheat in the center, across which the letters *P of H* are printed. They stand for Patrons of Husbandry, originally the official name of the organization, while the seven sides represent the seven founders, Kelley and six associates, and also the seven categories of Grange members from Junior Grange

(for five- to fourteen-year-olds) to the national body head-
quartered in Washington, D.C.

In the approximately forty states where Grange chapters
exist, some units run their own agricultural fairs. The Grange
also sponsors horticultural displays, food booths, art, craft,
and entertainment shows, and community service projects at
state, county, and local fairs.

Back in the days of Elkanah Watson, most farmers would
have scoffed at the idea of sending their sons to college to
learn to be farmers. On-the-farm training, from early child-
hood, was the way sons and daughters gained the necessary
knowledge and skills for a life similar to that of their parents.
Yet, only forty years later, in 1855, America's first state agricultural college was opened at East Lansing, Michigan.

Today there are numerous well-attended agricultural colleges and vocational schools across the country, despite the
fact that a small percentage of the population is now involved
in farm production for the American consumer. Many young
people with nonfarm backgrounds are now showing a deep
interest in agricultural careers, perhaps because of the impend-
ing world food shortage and the concern with preservation of
our environment in an industrial age.

Out of the agricultural colleges that began to be established
in the mid-nineteenth century have come the farm and home
extension services and the agricultural experiment stations,
their influence stretching like a fine network into the most
remote farm households through agricultural bulletins, traveling extension workers, county agents, and, of course, state
and county fairs.

The agricultural experiment station, supported by Federal
and state money and based usually at a state agricultural

Apple and plum varieties developed and grown in New York State

college, is the pioneer in all matters relating to better production founded on meticulous scientific study. An example of how an agricultural experiment station interacts with a state fair can be seen in New York, where the Cornell University station, established in 1892, recently introduced eight new fruit varieties at the New York State Fair.

Two new kinds of peaches, three types of grapes, a new plum, apple, and strawberry variety—the result of twenty years of careful plant breeding and experimentation—were considered ready for presentation to farmers, commercial processors and distributors, and the general public. The new fruits were displayed at the fair along with information about the special attributes that make them well-suited to New York

State growing conditions, their promise in terms of quality and yield, and their suitability for canning, freezing, or other processing. A fruit specialist from the experiment station remained on hand at the exhibit throughout the run of the fair to answer questions about the new varieties and about fruit growing in general.

As the director of the New York State Fair has said, the fair that features agricultural events in their rightful place is "another kind of school," disseminating top-quality information to farmers and offering a "capsule view" of the agricultural process to a generation of Americans that, for the most part, no longer has any roots in rural America. For them, the state fair may be the only place where it can still see "a chick hatched, a cow milked, a calf born."

4

Arts,
Crafts,
and
Homemaking

If you can bake a better biscuit, sew a straighter seam, tool leather, refinish furniture, enamel jewelry, or paint on china, you are invited each year to partake of prizes at your state, county, or other local fair. These are just a few of the premium, or prize, divisions that fall into the category of arts, crafts, and homemaking.

When Elkanah Watson brought "household arts" into the Berkshire County Fair of 1813, he was looking for a way to enlist the interests of farmers' wives in fair activities, so that going to the fair, whether as an exhibitor or a spectator, could become a family enterprise. Watson felt, too, that preserving fruits, canning vegetables, spinning flax, wool, and cotton and converting them into "useful and ornamental" objects were all "patriotic" duties.

He was right, of course, for in post-Revolutionary America using native materials well and inventively and cutting down on foreign imports was essential to the economic well-being and continuing independence of the nation.

In Watson's time, manufactured goods for the home were nearly all manufactured *in* the home. Commercial canning processes, for example, were not even known in the United

60

States until about 1815, and the first tin cans did not come into use until 1825. Necessities, from baked goods to bed linens, from petticoats to hearth rugs, were produced from "scratch" in farmhouse kitchens. And, in keeping with the traditional female role in Western society, most of these articles of domestic manufacture were created by women.

Today many of the household arts of Watson's day are practiced not out of necessity but as enjoyable activities that reflect love of craftsmanship and deep creative interests. Sometimes home talents give birth to vocations and even small businesses such as food catering, custom needlework, or the selling of home-crafted objects.

At modern fairs, the household arts category has expanded beyond cookery and needlework to include a broad range of

A needlecrafts exhibit
at the New York State Fair's Art and Home Center

The fine arts and photography exhibit
at Connecticut's Bethlehem Fair

workshop hobbies such as woodworking, metal sculpture, pottery making, mosaic tiling, jewel cutting, scale model making,
and bookbinding, as well as photography and fine arts. Both
men and women exhibit in these premium divisions. Yet, surprisingly, a number of fairs around the country still lump these
activities into their Women's Department and house the prize
entries in exhibits in their Women's Building.

It is incorrect, of course, to associate household arts with
women exclusively, and many fairs use terms like Homemaking Arts or Home Center. Just as women are beginning to
compete more in agricultural events, men are starting to enter
their coffee cakes and casseroles, handwoven textiles, and creative stitchery at fairs. After all, when a 300-pound (male)
professional football tackle writes a book about needlepoint

for men—as has happened—it becomes possible to imagine a man being chosen as Homemaker of the Year at a future state fair.

The title of Homemaker of the Year is offered at the Southeastern Fair, held annually in Atlanta, Georgia. Similar awards are given at some other state fairs as well. The Atlanta fair, which runs for ten days in late September and early October, is billed as "Georgia's largest annual event." Like most state fairs, it is the state's most important public festival, its dates being as familiar and special as those of Thanksgiving and Christmas. The Southeastern Fair has been in existence since 1914.

On the day of the fair that is set aside as Homemaker's Day the winning homemaker, selected from 100,000 Georgia women, is honored along with ten runners-up from each of Georgia's congressional districts. Choosing and crowning the top winner has been a fair highlight since 1954, with the title sometimes bestowed by the United States' president's wife or daughter or by a cabinet member's wife. An engraved silver tray and a week's vacation with her family on Georgia's offshore Jekyll Island are among the winner's rewards. More important, during the year that she wears her crown the Georgia fair's top homemaker functions as a sort of goodwill ambassador on the home-economics circuit, appearing before farming, women's, and civic groups as an inspiration and as an example of all that is commendable in American family life.

Such high honors are not the goal of the average fair entrant, who is usually in it for the pure joy of winning—and the token but nevertheless important prize money. Although the total amount of premium money set aside for cash awards has grown by leaps and bounds since the early days of the agricultural fair, it is the idea of achievement rather than the

The jubilant winner accepting the Southeastern Fair's
Georgia Homemaker of the Year award

size of the awards that prods most contestants and exhibitors toward excellence.

At the State Fair of Texas, held every October in Dallas—the largest fair in the country—$11,000 in premium money is offered in the arts, crafts, and homemaking category. However, this sum is spread among first-, second-, and third-place winners in dozens of subdivisions that are further broken down into more than one thousand different "classes."

For example, prizes of $5, $3, and $2 are offered in the Texas state fair's candy-making contest. The kinds of home-made candy to be submitted fall into seven different classes: chocolate fudge, other kinds of fudge, divinity, pralines, mints, hand-dipped chocolates, nut brittles. If there are three winners in every class, $70 of prize money is awarded. This is equal to the amount of prize money awarded to all of the entrants at the Berkshire County Fair in 1811!

However, we must remember that the Berkshire County Fair lasted one day and attracted 3000 people, while the giant Texas fair runs for over two weeks and its attendance re-peatedly exceeds three million. The fairgrounds and many of their buildings were established in 1936 for the 100th anni-versary celebration of Texan independence from Mexico. The fair has its own large state-fair park, as well-kept and attrac-tive as that of some of the great world's fairs of modern times. The famed Cotton Bowl stadium sits in the midst of the fair-grounds, and towering skyward in the very heart of the fair park looms the immense booted and hatted figure, in red-checked shirt and Levis, of Big Tex, fifty-two feet high and surely the tallest Texas cowboy in the world.

Because of the size and prosperity of the State Fair of Texas, the activities in the arts, crafts, and homemaking division are broader and more varied than at many of the average-sized state fairs. As at most of today's fairs, the major portion of the prize money comes out of the fair treasury, mainly from the rental of commercial exhibit space and from gate receipts. The state or other community, business and industry, and some private agencies generally make up the balance either in money or gift prizes. At the Texas Fair, in addition to the usual cook-ing, needlework, and hobby divisions, prizes are offered in such categories as table settings (first prize $10), pumpkin-carving,

Christmas-tree trimming ($25 first prize), and original, hand-crafted holiday articles in *fifty* different classes ranging from decorated Easter eggshells to Christmas stockings.

Texas regional food traditions are expressed in the El Chico chili contest which has two classes—"with beans" and "without beans." And the baking and home-canned vegetable contests include classes for such local specialties as sweet-potato pie and black-eyed peas. As in the case of all prepared-food entries at state and county fairs, written recipes must accompany each dish, for the basic idea is not only to do well enough to win a prize but to give others the opportunity to achieve the same level of performance. They, in turn, may try for even greater accomplishment at next year's fair.

Excellence on the amateur level is complemented, at most larger fairs around the country, with displays of professional talents and abilities. At the Texas state fair, the daily events in the arts, crafts, and homemaking department include demonstrations of china painting and clockmaking, metal sculpture and Indian crafts, quilting bees and cooking shows, as well as a professional fashion show with clothes contributed by major manufacturers. The fashion show, so elaborately staged that it approaches a musical-theater production, is presented free several times daily.

Examples like these from the professional world serve to introduce the nonprofessional fair contestant to stimulating ideas and to set more ambitious goals for them. At the same time, these teaching demonstrations and shows provide inviting entertainment for all.

Another fair with a flourishing arts, crafts, and homemaking department is the New York State Fair which runs for one week, usually in late August and early September, at Syracuse. Housed since 1934 in its own large, Colonial-style brick build-

A New York State Fair weaving demonstration

ing, the Art and Home Center is a magnet for a great many of the 600,000 fairgoers who attend each year. Aside from the displays in the creative arts competitions, ranging from ceramics to stuffed animals and from macrame to decoupage, there are always daily events of interest.

In the glass-enclosed food-judging booth on the main floor, home economists and other cooking authorities taste and rate the day's entries in the culinary arts competition—a bit of wine jelly, a sliver of applesauce cake, just a fleck or two of peach piecrust. In the air-conditioned demonstration kitchen, with its ceiling-mirrored work counter, walk-in pantry, and informal dining areas, an audience of 200 can watch five cooking shows a day for the run of the fair.

Home economists from the food industry, from colleges and extension services, from magazine staffs and government agen-

cies demonstrate a wide variety of food-preparation techniques and offer free literature and recipes. During a single fair day, they may present breadmaking and fondue cookery, crepes and omelets, home-canning hints, and how to prepare wild game for the pot or freezer.

Opposite, above: Tasting and rating baked goods
in New York State Fair's Art and Home Center
Opposite, below: Step-by-step cake baking
demonstrated at the New York State Fair
Below: Budget-wise ways with meat,
demonstrated by a home economist at the New York State Fair

Another popular gathering place at the New York State Fair's Art and Home Center is the theater auditorium, in which fashion shows, slide shows, documentary films, and special programs of interest to homemakers, hobbyists, and consumers are presented all day every day. Through these approaches, fairs build bridges between experts and those who would like to be informed, inspired, and educated to new skills and better techniques.

Modeling sewing projects at a New York State Fair fashion show

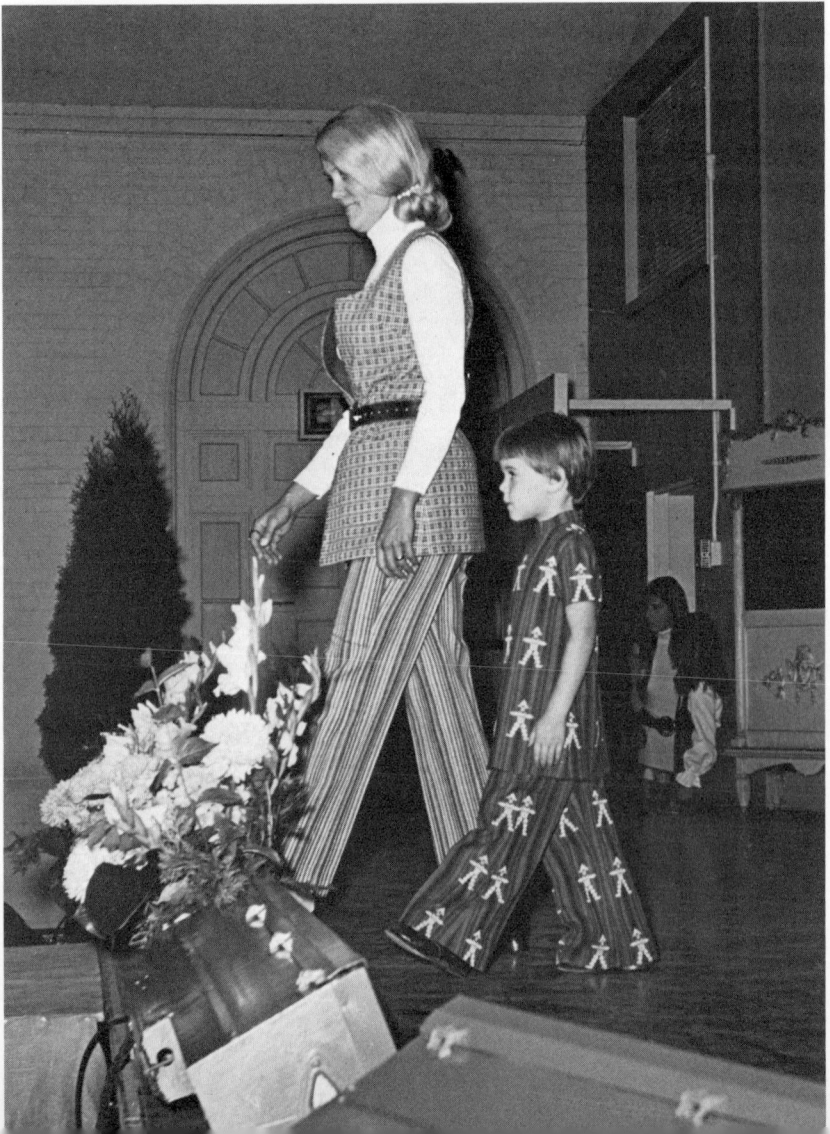

Pride in America's older citizens was expressed at the very first Berkshire County Fair in 1810. According to Elkanah Watson's approach, fairs were no longer to be mere market-places but were to serve as showcases for the best the nation had to offer. By honoring the oldest man in the county, Watson was paying homage to all those earnest and hardworking folk who had contributed so much energy and know-how to the general betterment over the course of years.

Today most state fairs and many county fairs show deep interest in providing special programs for senior citizens. Older people's activities generally fall into the scope of the arts, crafts, and homemaking departments. There are prizes established for the work of men and women of sixty-five, or seventy, or older, in knitting and crocheting, sewing, quilting, rug making, hobby crafts, painting, and photography. For example, at the New York State Fair, there have been exhibits of imaginatively designed and exquisitely executed dollhouses, created by grandfathers for their grandchildren, and of intricately patterned patchwork quilts made by grandmothers for the trousseaus of their granddaughters.

Often one day of the fair is set aside as Senior Citizens' day and throughout the run of the fair there are special coffee hours, songfests, square-dancing contests, free tours and demonstrations, as well as a comfortable, shady outdoor sitting place with benches for older fairgoers.

Fairs are a mecca, too, for older people who are not able to participate directly. Civic and religious groups often arrange day outings by bus, at special reduced rates, to visit county or state fairs that are within comfortable traveling distance. Connecticut's spacious and handsome Danbury Fair, which runs for ten days in late September and early October, attracts droves of older weekday visitors, who arrive on orga-

Older fairgoers enjoying the Danbury Fair
from the comfort of the fairground sightseeing bus

nized tours from as far away as New Jersey, Pennsylvania, Massachusetts, and upper New York State.

While fairs do much to set young people on the road to achievement and excellence, to promote the work and recreation activities of adult men and women, and to celebrate the accomplishments of older people, there is another special plus: the way in which fairs bring people together in behind-the-scenes activities. At the New York State Fair's Art and Home Center, for example, students from high schools and colleges are employed to assist the food judges in the cookery competitions, to help set up the craft exhibits, to keep the fashion shows running smoothly, and to cooperate in the background work of the demonstration kitchen. This shared effort among people of all ages and of varied skills and experience, and the instilling of good work habits in youth, are some of the most valuable of the benefits to be derived from fairs.

5

Youth
and
Vocational
Activities

The Utah State Fair, a ten-day event that takes place every September in Salt Lake City, recently held an essay contest for schoolchildren. Asked to tell about what they had learned from their visit to the fair, one young grade-schooler wrote, "I learned that a pig could be one of the prettiest animals in the world." A second child wrote, "I learned water beds are comfortable," and another declared, "Well, I never thought that Utah had so many counties."

Young people have, of course, been going to fairs since the days of Elkanah Watson. Farmers' sons, in particular, were taken along to the early county fairs to help feed and maintain the livestock that was to be entered for judging. But a separate youth category for fair entries did not come along until rather late in the day.

Around 1900, various farmers' groups began to sponsor agricultural clubs for boys and girls. Some of these club leaders must have taken their idea from the Grange, formed back in 1867. At any rate, clubs for farm youth sprang up independently in various parts of the country. They centered on activities like poultry raising, corn growing, and fruit-and-vegetable canning.

The first official youth exhibit on record took place at the Louisiana Purchase Centennial Exposition in 1904. This was a world's fair, held at Saint Louis, Missouri, to celebrate the 100th anniversary of the purchase of the Louisiana Territory from France. Forty-two states and fifty-three foreign countries took part in this international event. The theme of the exposition was education; the explanation of processes and the application of science in everyday life were declared to be of greater importance than the finished products themselves.

Accordingly, an important feature of the exposition was a Palace of Agriculture. There over 8000 farm youths from the State of Illinois exhibited corn-growing projects that they had been developing in their agricultural clubs, projects dealing with the improvement of seed strains, planting techniques, and crop yield.

Spurred by this example, and encouraged by funding from the Department of Agriculture in 1914, school and civic leaders began organizing clubs on a national basis. By 1924, the name 4-H had come into general use, and the clubs were becoming involved in state and county fair activities all around the country.

The 4-H symbol is a green four-leaf clover with a large H printed on each leaf. Head, heart, hands, and health are what the four H's stand for, as expressed in the pledge taken by new members of the organization:

I pledge
   My head to clearer thinking,
   My heart to greater loyalty,
   My hands to larger service,
   My health to better living,
      for my club, my community, and my country.

A 4-H craft demonstration
in the New York State Fair's Youth Building

Aside from their participation in fairs, 4-H members, who must be between ten and twenty years old, have regular year-round club meetings and work on both individual and group projects. Members select their projects from areas ranging from agriculture, forestry, and wildlife to crafts and home-making skills, and from personal health and community safety programs to money management and career studies. For group projects, there are lectures, discussions, demonstrations, documentary films, and recreational activities that take place in connection with the monthly meetings.

Reporting on individual projects, planning for a club's exhibit at a local or state fair, and learning democratic processes and procedures through the operation of the club itself are all part of 4-H work. Prizes and awards for individual and group projects are given by farm, business, and civic organizations and range from blue ribbons to college scholarships. Today clubs exist in large cities as well as rural townships, and 4-H is also an international idea, with clubs in a number of world nations and an international youth-exchange program.

Fairs act as annual showcases for other youth organizations, too. The Future Farmers of America, formed during the 1920's for young people studying agriculture as a vocation on the high-school level, is almost as active as 4-H in fairs today. FFA is similar to 4-H except that it is restricted to boys whose interests lie mainly in farming careers. The first state-wide association of these agricultural-students' clubs was the Future Farmers of Virginia, established in 1926. Two years later the national organization was founded, and today it is administered and partially funded by the Federal Department of Health, Education, and Welfare.

FFA beginners usually start out as high-school freshmen, doing small-crop growing or chick-breeding projects. Some chapters use the "pig chain" or "calf chain" system for starter projects. The chapter gives the club member a female pig or calf to raise. The animal's first female offspring is then given to the chapter to pass on to another young FFA member for his starter project. FFA youths may continue their membership until three years after leaving high school or until reaching the age of twenty-one, whichever comes later.

In addition to agricultural subjects, Future Farmers apply themselves to related matters like nature and wildlife study,

Minding the calves at the FFA and 4-H Dairy Club
combined exhibit at a local fair in Connecticut

tractor operation, power- and hand-tool skills, and farm machinery repair. The FFA emblem is a yellow cross section of
an ear of corn, showing a scalloped border of kernels. On this
ground, an owl symbolizing knowledge, a plow symbolizing
labor, and a rising sun symbolizing the promise of the future
are depicted. An eagle perched atop this emblem indicates
FFA's national status.

Other, newer club groups, such as Future Homemakers of
America and Future Business Leaders of America, also participate in state and county fairs. FHA, formed in 1945 and
devoted to home, family, and community activities, works
closely with home economics groups and consumer organizations, volunteers to assist with young children, and hosts youth

groups from foreign countries. FBLA is geared to high-school and college students interested in careers in business, industry, or business teaching.

Today's state and county fairs literally open their doors wide to youth. The New York State Fair and the North Carolina State Fair, among others, have a policy of admitting children under twelve free at all times. In addition, many fairs set aside a special Youth Day on which all young people under the age of sixteen are admitted free. Some fairs feature days on which 4-H, FFA, FHA, Junior Grange, Scouts, Y groups, and other youth-organization members are admitted free or at reduced rates, and all fairs welcome school classes in groups.

Florida's Dade County Youth Fair, at Miami, and Boise's Western Idaho Fair both emphasize youth achievement as a permanent theme and offer such attractions as young people's photography and fashion shows, teen concerts, and free barbecues for junior livestock exhibitors. Aside from the learning, creativity, inspiration, and career guidance that fairs offer to young people, fair planners today realize that youth is big business both for the present and the future. "Catch 'em while they're young," is the creed of most fair managements.

Once inside the fairground gates, every young person, whether toddler or older teen-ager, can find something to enjoy. Many small children from nonfarm backgrounds make their first acquaintance with animals at the Petting Zoo, Mother Goose Barnyard, Red Barn, or similarly named exhibit where lambs and kids, calves and piglets, ponies and

Opposite, above: Learning about baby animals
at a fair's Mother Goose Barnyard
Opposite, below: Feeding goats with approved animal food
at the Danbury Fair's petting zoo

First time at the fair for a youthful visitor

donkeys, and small cuddly animals like chicks, ducks, kittens, puppies, and rabbits may be admired, touched, and sometimes fed with approved animal food. At some fairs, an adult costumed as a Mother Goose or another storybook character is present to lift a kitten or rabbit so that a child can stroke it, or to answer questions about the habits of farm animals.

Drawing children directly into fair competitions begins at an early age nowadays. The State Fair of Texas sponsors a Freckle Contest for anyone old enough to exhibit an outstanding crop of freckles. Entrants are divided into classes: up through the age of seven, eight to sixteen years, and sixteen and over. Twins and Look-Alike contests, at the Texas fair are open to toddlers and up. In the Twins Contest, prizes are awarded for "most alike" and "least alike" pairs, while Look-Alike prizes are given to mother-daughter pairs and other parent-child combinations with the strongest resemblance to one another. In the fair's Bubblegum Contest, the youngest group is the six- to nine-year-old class, followed by children aged ten to thirteen, fourteen to sixteen, and lastly seventeen and over. Apparently the Texas judges feel that blowing outsize gum bubbles is a highly specialized business.

The New York State Fair features a spelling bee for winners of county-fair spelling contests from all around the state. The premium money, which is put up by the state fair, is high, a total of $325, with $100 awarded to the first-prize winner. The runners-up receive suitable gifts of dictionaries (presented by a publishing company), as well as smaller cash prizes. In the arts and recreation area, the New York fair sponsors a variety of activities for youth: the Auburn Children's Theater "act wagon" with its daily presentations of children's plays, clown acts, and puppet shows; the Fantasyland fairground paint-in encouraging on-the-spot originality and creativity, with paints and canvas donated by the fair; schoolchildren's art exhibits like the Buffalo Youth in Art show at the Art and Home Center; and competitions for baton-twirling drum majors and majorettes, and high-school marching bands.

However, young people participate in a much wider range

of fair activities. The New York State Fair's Youth Building is the scene of almost an entire fair in miniature. There most of the 4-H, FFA, and FHA exhibits are installed: home-decorating and home-improvement design displays; textiles and clothing, featuring attractive, well-constructed dresses, sportswear, and other garments; cookies, breads, cakes, and international foods; and food-and-nutrition science projects.

There, too, 4-H'ers display their egg-and-poultry science exhibits, dairy products, fruits and vegetables, flower and landscaping projects, and natural resources projects on forestry, fish and wildlife, geology, and environment awareness.

On the second floor of the Youth Building, modestly priced, supervised dormitory accommodations are available to young people who have brought livestock to the fair or must otherwise remain with their exhibits over a period of days. Near the Youth Building are the livestock barns where 4-H dairy

Opposite, above: Thumbelina puppet show
at the Auburn Children's Theater, New York State Fair
Opposite, below: On-the-spot creativity
at the New York State Fair's Fantasyland Paint-In
Below: A teen-ager tending his horses
at the barns near the Youth Building

A small-engine troubleshooting contest
for future farmers at the New York State Fair

cattle, livestock, and horses are judged. In addition, there are
contests for sheepshearing, dogs' obedience training, and horse-
back riding; there is a 4-H polo tournament; and there are
FFA tractor-safety demonstrations and FFA farm-engine
troubleshooting competitions.

For young people, in particular, a fair is much more than
a place to win a prize for a smile full of freckles, the best
batch of yeast rolls, top horsemanship, or a well-bred Poland
China pig. A fair is a community showcase to which youth
makes a very substantial contribution, largely through the
work of national youth organizations like 4-H and FFA. In
addition, a really responsible, community-oriented fair pays
youth back many times over, beyond the reward of an excel-
lent entry or a winning skill, even beyond the opportunities
for learning from one another and the valuable experiences
of working with others and learning how to communicate with
the public. A good state or county fair is also a marketplace
in which young people can shop for a future.

A state fisheries exhibit may set a country youngster to thinking of a career in marine biology; a medical association's careers booth may draw a small-town girl's attention to the not-impossible dream of becoming a doctor; a city child may respond so overwhelmingly to a state agricultural-college display that he will decide to become a stock breeder; and a farm child may be so intrigued with a NASA space-station model that he will set his course for the stars.

Good fairs, in fact, reveal a glimpse of the future itself and suggest some of its possibilities to youth.

6

Midway
and
Entertainment
Events

Cotton candy and crazy rides, houses of horror, halls of mirrors, and the ballyhoo of sideshow barkers. . . . No fair visitor, young or old, country-born or city-bred, seems able to resist the razzle-dazzle and hurly-burly of the carnival midway.

Circuslike entertainment at fairs goes back, at least, to the market fairs of the Middle Ages with their tumblers and clowns, fire-eaters and tightrope walkers. But in the young United States, particularly in New England, fairs tended to be austere. Amusements, if they existed, consisted mainly of simple games and contests in which fairgoers participated, parades and marching bands, and, at some fairs, horse races and occasional fireworks displays.

Throughout the nineteenth century, the commercial traveling carnival was not a feature of the state and county agricultural fair, as it is today. Even at the Philadelphia Centennial Exposition of 1876, which played host to over eight million visitors, amusements were not featured. The exposition, which was held in celebration of the 100th anniversary of the signing of the Declaration of Independence, drew exhibitors from more than thirty foreign nations, so it was really an international, or world's, fair, one of the earliest held in the United States. Perhaps the new scientific and industrial miracles displayed—the printing press, the sewing machine, and the refrigerator car, the telephone, the telegraph, and the typewriter—were entertainment enough for the fascinated crowds that moved among them.

Interestingly enough, it was a New Englander, born in Bethel, Connecticut, in 1810, who developed the traveling amusement show into big business. His name was Phineas T. Barnum, and he organized his Greatest Show on Earth in 1871. Later he was one of the proprietors of the famed Barnum and Bailey Circus.

American circuses and fairs probably came together for the first time when Barnum, who was president of his local Fairfield County Agricultural Society, loaned a tent to a group of Connecticut farmers and manufacturers in neighboring Danbury for a town fair. This was in October of 1869, the opening year of the Danbury Fair. Barnum was already a prosperous showman at the time, having exhibited and toured the midget General Tom Thumb and the singer Jenny Lind, known as the Swedish Nightingale.

But the fair that truly introduced sideshows and other amusement-park features was the World's Columbian Exposition held at Chicago in 1893. This was another world's fair. Like the Philadelphia Centennial Exposition of 1876, its purpose was not only to commemorate the past but to proclaim man's progress in the arts, sciences, and industry, and it was also international in scope. However, like other world's fairs that began to take place both in the United States and abroad in the mid-nineteenth century, the international exposition had borrowed its show-and-exhibition idea from the humbler agricultural fair.

The theme of the Chicago Columbian Exposition was the celebration of the 400th anniversary of Columbus's discovery of America in 1492. It was planned, of course, that the fair should take place in 1892, but the task of organizing it was so great that it did not open until May 1, 1893. Among the carnival attractions of the exposition were a trained wild-animal act imported from Germany through the efforts of P. T. Barnum, an exotic veiled Eastern dancer known as Little Egypt, and the world's very first Ferris wheel.

The Ferris wheel of the Midway Plaisance, as the fair's amusement area was called, was enormous. It rose 264 feet into the air, about the height of a 30-story building, and each

The first Ferris wheel, at the Chicago world's fair of 1893

of its 36 cars held 60 passengers, a total capacity of 2160 persons! The wheel's inventor was an American mechanical engineer named George Washington Gale Ferris.

The Columbian Exposition's Ferris wheel had an impressive safety record, but it was doomed to extinction because of its monstrous size and weight. Its foundation had to be sunk into a 15-foot-deep bed of concrete, and it required two 500-horsepower steam engines to turn it. After an appearance at the Louisiana Purchase Centennial Exposition, held in Saint Louis, Missouri, in 1904, the original Ferris wheel was demolished and sold for scrap metal.

However, the popularity of the Ferris wheel was established, not only in the United States but all over the world, for it had enthralled exposition visitors and exhibitors alike. For the most part, smaller, portable wheels came into demand. The early 1900's saw Ferris wheels hitting the carnival trail as part of truck shows and railway-car shows, visiting both large and small fairs around the country.

The international exposition had borrowed its exhibition-of-products idea largely from the American agricultural fair; now the "big expo" returned the favor by offering new entertainment ideas, including the very use of the word *midway* to denote an avenue of amusements. These amusements, it was soon noted, could be adapted very successfully to the agricultural fair. And the time was ripe, for by the 1920's the American economy was booming and jazz-age Americans were beginning to demand livelier entertainment and brighter lights at state and county fairs.

Today a number of good-sized carnival outfits traverse the United States and Canada each year from early summer until late fall, playing fair dates. Among the largest of the big-business carnival shows are the James E. Strates show and

Royal American Shows. Both travel in railway cars, an idea developed by Barnum as an improvement over the old horse-and-wagon road shows, and both boast a "mile-long midway," although it is a curving or zigzagging mile, depending on the fairground. Both carnival outfits were founded in the early 1920's by fathers of the present owners. Other major outfits include Amusements of America, a huge truck show operated by five brothers as five self-contained units, two or more of which can be combined for really large fair dates, and Gooding's Million Dollar Midway, which boasts that it is large enough to play three major fairs at one time.

Expanding from its fifteen-car show of the 1920's, Royal American Shows now travels in an eighty-six-car train and has played the third largest fair in the United States, the Minnesota State Fair, with its annual attendance of nearly one and one-half million. Goodings has played the next-to-largest Ohio State Fair, which attracts nearly two and one-quarter million fairgoers. However, the largest United States

The carnival midway, a must at modern-day fairs of all sizes

fair, the State Fair of Texas, operates its own permanent amusement park.

Thirty or forty belly-pitching rides can be found nowadays on most good-sized midways. The older and more sedate merry-go-round (invented in Europe in about 1800) and the Ferris wheel have been joined by Sky Wheels and Sky Divers, Rock-o-Planes and Tilt-a-Whirls, the Octopus, the Scrambler, the Rampage, and the Twister, among others. Small children enjoy the Kiddieland rides and the Space Cushion, a plastic-domed "jumping hut" with a springy, resilient "floor" that gives a trampoline effect. As all fair and amusement operators know, it is important to have a ride for every age and taste, and to keep new thrills coming.

Freaks and other carnival sideshow attractions, and games of chance and skill, have not always been tasteful or honest. Grotesque human and animal freaks, vulgar girly shows, and rigged games of pokerino, bottle pitch, and duck pond, among others, have been offenders on fair midways for years. Un-

Kiddieland ride, with Space Cushion in background

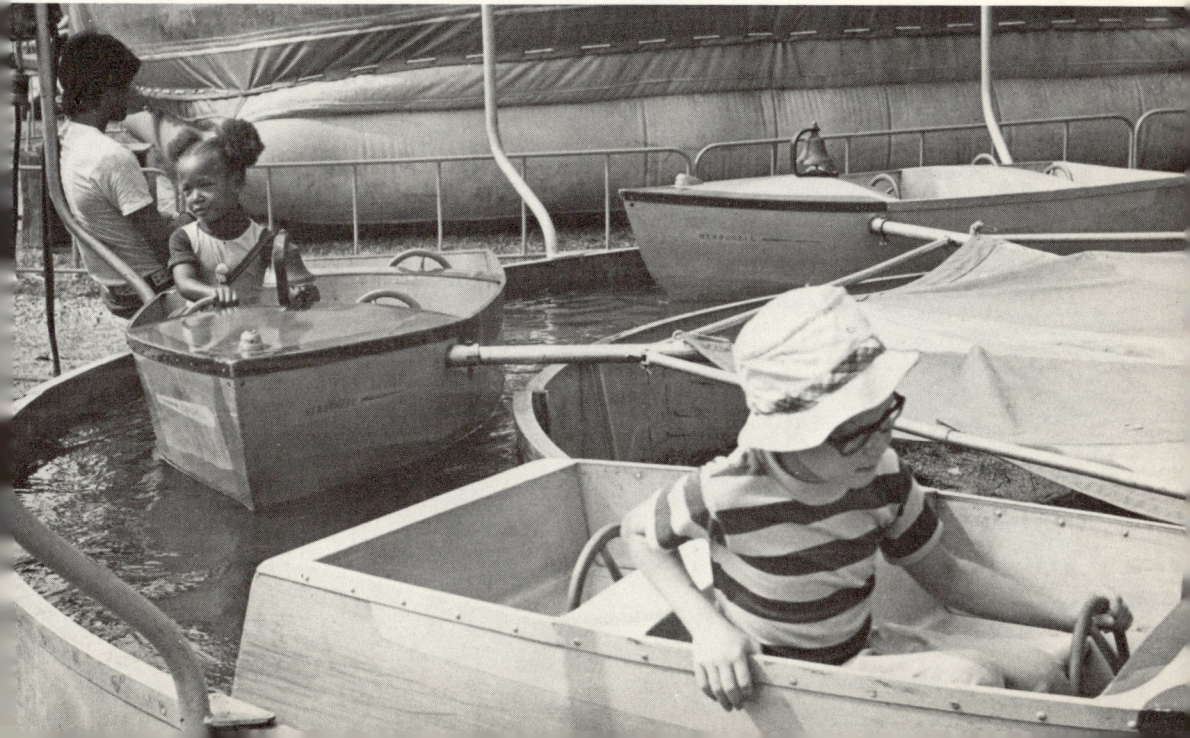

scrupulous carnival owners and irresponsible fair operators too often showed a belittling attitude toward the "marks" and "rubes" who came to the fair on their once-a-year holidays, determined to let off some steam. If the customers were cheated and ill-treated, the "carnies" reasoned, it was their own fault. They operated on the principle of "let the buyer beware."

Today most carnival outfits realize that consumers are better-informed and that fair patrons are made up largely of family groups looking for suitable entertainment for all their members. They know that dishonest or tasteless practices will be reported to fair managers, who will cancel the carnival's engagement the next year. In fact, as movies and even television networks become more daring in what they present, the one-time evils of the midway seem to grow much more innocent and to fall more and more into the category of "good clean fun."

In tailoring the midways to meet higher standards of good taste, some fair managements have asked that carnivals eliminate human freak shows as being unusually distressing to young or impressionable fair visitors. Carnival people respond with the argument that midgets and giants, 700-pound men and women, armless and legless "seal" people born with flippers rather than normal limbs, bearded ladies, and other of nature's mistakes would have little or no other way of earning their livings.

The very existence of freak shows in carnivals and circuses also produces self-made freaks such as tattooed men and women, sword-swallowers, and contortionists. Illusionary horror shows have usually done well at carnivals, along with freak shows. Famous "acts," whose secrets must be bought from their inventors, include the transformation of girl into gorilla and the decapitated living woman. These amazingly

Animal freak sideshow at a small rural fair in Connecticut

convincing performances are, as might be expected, all done with mirrors.

While some midways have toned down their human freak shows, animal freaks and monsters are still popular, particularly at the smaller fairs that draw many country people. Farm families are especially curious about a hairless cow or a five-legged deer, and everyone seems intrigued with viewing a live two-headed turtle or a 1300-pound alligator.

We may wonder why today's fairgoing public, with its neighborhood movie theaters and home television screens, seems as interested in amusement-park rides and sideshows as people did in the days when carnivals at fairs provided the only entertainment of the year. The answer is that picture screens can offer only spectator experiences—and mechanically produced ones at that. The tug of participatory and direct experience is a strong one for most of us.

Even the shivery sensation of sinking 250 feet from the top of the Parachute Jump, the frustration of trying to toss a small ball into a large peach basket and missing every time, the spine-chilling walk through the wax museum, and the revolting sight of the snake woman wrestling with her denful of writhing reptiles are preferable to having no direct experiences at all. This is one reason why the amusement-park idea has prospered since the 1920's and why the present is rapidly becoming an era of permanent super-amusement parks based on the Disneyland model.

In addition to their carnival-operated midways, most state and county fairs offer an increasing number of individual spectacle and thrill events. On the evening before the opening of Georgia's Southeastern Fair, a giant balloon parade marches the length of Atlanta's famed Peachtree Street. And throughout the run of the fair, there is a nightly fireworks extravaganza on the fairgrounds. The Georgia fair also features the massive water-fountain spectacle, also seen at other larger fairs, known as Dancing Waters. Controlled from an organ-like console, thousands of gallons of water, powered by nineteen motors, are shot through four thousand jets to heights of twenty to forty feet. Swaying, swirling, and swishing, the waters "dance" tangos, waltzes, ballets, and modern rhythms, all to the accompaniment of music and ever-changing colored lights. Dancing Waters performances are given six times daily at the Georgia fair.

As in an earlier day, many fairs present horse races, horse-

Opposite, above: Atlanta's giant balloon parade
held on the eve of the opening of the Southeastern Fair
Opposite, below: Horseracing events,
traditional entertainment at state and county fairs

jump shows, and rodeos. The latter are especially popular at Western and Midwestern fairs. For thrill seekers of the motorized age, there are stock-car and other auto races, as well as auto daredevil acts like the Demolition Derby and the hell drivers, with their seventy-mile-per-hour jumps and acrobatics. Motorcycle races draw peak crowds, as do wall-of-death acts in which the audience sits around the lip of a deep cup-shaped well watching one or even two crazily tilted cyclists rapidly circling the vertical inner walls. As if this were not breathtaking enough, some cyclists perform this feat riding backwards or with no hands!

Thrill events at fairs take to the sky, too, with helicopter acrobatics. Aerial stunts are performed from a trapeze platform dangling from a hovering, teetering, and sometimes swift-moving helicopter and include such hair-raisers as the "heel catch" and the "hangman's neck spin." Helicopter acrobatics are often performed for an after-dark grandstand audience with the spotlighted performer dressed in a dazzling fluorescent costume.

One effect of the television age on fairs has been the demand for personal appearances by performers who are well known, often on an international scale, through their frequent presence on the home screen or their popularity on musical recordings. Most larger fairs top off their beauty contests, square- and folk-dance performances, and the acts of their local talent-hunt winners, with stars of country-and-Western and rock music, big-name comedians, actors, musicians, and

Opposite, above: Thrills and smashes with auto daredevils at the Demolition Derby, New York State Fair
Opposite, below: Dave Merrifield, helicopter acrobatic artist, performing at a state fair

singers from the current top-rated TV shows. The cost of such entertainment comes high, but fair managers say they can see the results at the gate, as fairgoers react enthusiastically to that once-in-a-lifetime chance for a live glimpse of one of the reigning entertainers of the day.

Above: Dancing the polka to the music
of a talented local group at the New York State Fair
Below: A top international recording star
packing in the crowds at the New York State Fair

Coping with cotton candy

Lastly, almost nobody leaves a fairground without eating something. Even well-intentioned fairground picnickers who have brought their own box lunches find it hard to resist the tempting sights and smells emanating from midway "grab stands" (no sitting down; a hamburger and a Coke on the run), from sellers of cotton candy and caramel popcorn, and from ice-cream vendors touting "walk-away sundaes" and other portable frozen delights.

The foods that probably have the greatest appeal at fairs are those with ethnic origins: Polish kielbasa sausage at the New York State Fair; Italian submarine sandwiches filled with meatballs and peppers in tomato sauce at the Danbury Fair; fried, wafflelike "funnel cakes" sprinkled with powdered sugar at the Kutztown Fair in Pennsylvania Dutch country; Mexican tacos and enchiladas at the State Fair of Texas. These are among the last remnants of American regionalism, and they can happily still be found at fairs in the era of the big-business, mass-produced, coast-to-coast hamburger.

Often the best food turns up at small country fairs, where the local fire department may have a booth selling hot, buttered sweet corn, freshly picked, shucked, and cooked, or where a women's civic or church club may be serving up squares of warm, freshly baked gingerbread with real country-fresh whipped cream.

Food prices are generally high at fairs, even for hot dogs, coffee, and soft drinks, for the fair visitor is a captive customer. But although pickings can vary from very poor to surprisingly good in terms of taste appeal and value for the money, the quality of most fair food is carefully supervised as to wholesomeness and cleanliness. No fair manager can risk the infecting tens of thousands of people with ptomaine poisoning.

Whatever the cost, the sense of taste, like all the other senses, is usually liberally indulged at state and county fairs, for most fairgoers feel that no visit is complete without sampling as many as possible of the pleasures of firsthand experience.

7

Special Exhibits

At a small country fair in Georgia, there is a working exhibit of an old sorghum mill used to crush sweet, sugarlike sorghum cane into syrup as in the rural South of a couple of generations ago. At a large county fair in the Midwest, there is a vividly mounted drug-abuse exhibit with accompanying information about the county's drug-prevention clinics. And two large state fairs in the heart of the American Southwest, surrounded by a landscape of oil derricks, are extraordinarily proud of their foreign-culture exhibits from countries as far off as Japan, Romania, India, Israel, Zaire, Peru, and the Soviet Union.

These exhibits relating to America's past, its challenging present, and to the world beyond American shores are examples of a growing awareness on the part of fair program planners. They realize that state, county, and even local fairs in the modern age must take on new responsibilities and functions if they are to continue to be both vital and inviting. They believe that American fairs can and should reflect a broad image of our society, our culture, and of the lives of our neighbors around the world.

This was not always the case. Back in the early days of the American agricultural fair, communities were small, town

meetings served to inform most people about community problems and projects, and the state, the nation, and the world
were rarely thought of because they had little noticeable impact on everyday affairs. The past was of such recent record
in those days that America's brief history was well-known to
most citizens. As to the machinery, implements, and other
museum relics of the past, they were not relics at all, for they
were still being used on the farms and in the households of
the day.

Even as late as the 1930's, if a fair ran the gamut from
agricultural, household arts, and youth department activities
to a carnival midway, and if it headlined a parade or fireworks
and an auto-stunt or other thrill show, it was considered to be
quite complete. In the middle of the nineteenth century, however, world's fairs had come into existence, and these took on
the role of bringing the world at large to the fair visitor. While
state and county fairs remained regional and detached, dwell-
ing mainly on matters related to agriculture and other traditional features, international fairs were appealing more and
more strongly to the imagination of the public. Even though
most people could not attend a famous exposition in Saint
Louis or Chicago or New York, they were beginning to hear
a great deal about them.

Among the earliest of these international expositions was
the London Crystal Palace Exhibition of 1851. It was designed
to gather together "the industry of all nations" and to show
products of both the arts and manufacturing from around
the world under a single roof. Its six million visitors saw,
among thousands of other displays, such new products from
the United States as the McCormick reaper and the Colt re-
peating pistol.

Fired with enthusiasm for Britain's great show, the New

Machinery Hall at the Philadelphia Centennial of 1876

York newspaper publisher, Horace Greeley, and a group of businessmen, promoted a Crystal Palace Exposition to be held in New York City in 1853. The domed glass-and-iron exhibit building (patterned after London's Crystal Palace) that was constructed in Bryant Park behind the New York Public Library proved to have a leaky roof beneath which a less-than-successful show of world arts and industry was housed. But at least the United States had played host to its first international exposition.

The Philadelphia Centennial Exposition of 1876, which followed, put the United States on the road to bigger and better world's fairs. In addition to viewing new inventions that would revolutionize transportation and communications throughout the world, millions of visitors strolled through the pavilions of exhibiting states and foreign countries, touching briefly on the lives of other Americans and of people of foreign lands. The Philadelphia Centennial also featured a collection of great art, brought together for the exposition and then permanently housed in the Philadelphia Museum of Art.

The World's Columbian Exposition at Chicago in 1893 drew twenty-one million visitors and was the largest American fair to date. It had its own Palace of Fine Arts, exhibited the Pullman sleeping car and the linotype machine, and introduced electricity on a grandiose scale to illuminate the canals and lagoons, and the glistening white, classical buildings of the fair park.

At the Louisiana Purchase Centennial Exposition of 1904, there was once again a Fine Arts Building, and there were impressive state and foreign pavilions. Germany exhibited its genius with industrial chemicals, and Japan dazzled fairgoers with its variety of manufactured articles. There was an exhibit describing the Philippines, to acquaint Americans with the island territory acquired by the United States in the recently fought Spanish-American War, and at the New York State Building cooking with electricity was an important new feature. But the most exciting addition to this world's fair was an auto show, a first occasion on which 100 of the amazing new vehicles that were to have such an impact on America's life-style were viewed by over twelve million disbelieving fair visitors.

World's fairs were doing a first-class job of reflecting world culture and registering industrial progress in an era when new scientific and technological achievements seemed to come along every other day. At the Panama-Pacific International Exposition of 1915, celebrating the opening of the Panama Canal, motion pictures were exhibited and the public was able to take airplane rides over San Francisco, where the fair was held.

In 1933-34, although the United States was in the depths of an economic depression, Chicago hosted a world's fair in honor of its one hundred years of growth and bravely termed the event a Century of Progress International Exposition. Prefabricated structures, functional architecture in simple, geometric forms, and the use of bright, clear colors showed the new strains of modernism and utilitarianism that were soon being incorporated into industrial design and were to become fashionable in daily living.

Poster for the 1933 Chicago World's Fair, ushering in new trends in design

This trend toward forms with strikingly sleek lines was even more noticeable at the New York World's Fair of 1939-40, which commemorated the 150th anniversary of President George Washington's inauguration in New York. The World of Tomorrow theme was symbolized by the globelike Perisphere and the tall, tapering, three-sided Trylon. The fair, with its forecasts of home television, abundant plastics and other synthetics, and new comfort-and-convenience features in everyday life, saw the country through the last days of the depression, but it ended with Europe already plunged into World War II and the United States on its way to entering the conflict.

World's fairs since the war, in both the United States and abroad, have reflected developments in the use of atomic energy and in space travel and have continued to show us the current state of our civilization illustrated through industry and the arts, through science and technology. It is also a comment on the state of our civilization that the 1974 world's fair at Spokane, Washington, chose the theme Celebrate Tomorrow's Fresh, New Environment, and that it geared many of its exhibits to the growing universal awareness of man's need to conserve and preserve the land, sea, and air about him. Perhaps this world's fair, Expo '74, closed a cycle, a century-long period of frenzied progress accompanied by an almost ruthless disregard for the limited resources of our planet.

While international fairs speak to us of the larger world in which we live, many of today's state and county fairs report to us on both our immediate interests and those of the rest of the nation and the world. Each year they reach many more people than any single international fair in the United States can hope to attract. And so they have adopted many ideas for special exhibits from world's fairs. At the same time, being smaller and more intimate than the international expositions, good state or county fairs put people in touch with the workings of their state and local governments and with key agencies in their communities.

At the New York State Fair, for example, visitors to the State Exhibits Building have a chance to learn and to ask questions about state programs concerning schools and hospitals, police work and power projects, transportation and employment services. And community awareness is further encouraged through the Volunteers in Action award, with a grand prize of $400 given to an organization within the state that has performed a unique service in an area such as health, education, conservation, community improvement, or preservation of some feature of the community's historical heritage.

A Hall of Health is an important and often lively feature at a state or county fair. Sometimes free chest X rays for tuberculosis are available, and simple laboratory tests are offered on the spot. There may be push-button exhibits that describe the workings of the human body and qualified people to talk to about community health services, hospitals, and careers in nursing and medicine. Usually there are slide shows, films, lectures, and free pamphlets about major national health problems such as heart disease, cancer, and alcoholism. Equally important at the local or regional fair, medical authorities can make a special effort to deal directly with those health conditions that pose a problem in the general vicinity but are perhaps less common elsewhere. Often local Red Cross chapters volunteer to demonstrate first-aid techniques, aquatic lifesaving, and standard safety practices, and a fair is always a good place to set up a blood-donor center.

Other science exhibits at fairs deal with pollution of the environment and offer suggestions for conservation of resources, cleaner air, proper disposal of wastes, and so forth. Natural history exhibits, often state-sponsored as is the one at the New York fair, show lifelike re-creations of the birds and animals of the state in dioramic displays. There is also an aquarium at the New York State Fair so that visitors can view the many fish varieties of the state's lakes and rivers.

Since the building of the Space Needle for Seattle's Century 21 Exposition in 1962, many state and county fairs have become increasingly space conscious. None have attempted anything so spectacular as the 600-foot-tall Space Needle tower with its revolving restaurant on top (which was left standing after the Seattle World's Fair closed), but many fairs have since featured exhibits related to space travel, including displays of moon-rock samples from the Apollo 12 lunar mission and a model of Skylab, America's first manned experimental space station.

Returning to more down-to-earth transportation marvels, the Los Angeles County Fair, at Pomona, California, possesses a monorail, a speedy, silent, single track railroad that whisks fairgoers from one end of the fairground to the other. The Los Angeles fair is the largest county fair in the United States, with an attendance of one and one-quarter million. Monorails have been used at world's fairs, including the Seattle fair, to transport passengers from downtown city locations to the fairgrounds. As to America's number one transportation vehicle, the State Fair of Texas actually incorporates a large, two-acre auto show in its Automobile Building, displaying gleaming new models of both American and imported cars for the coming year.

The space missile exhibit at the New York State Fair

An industry vital to the economy of the region is often highlighted at a state or county fair. The Southeastern Fair at Atlanta, Georgia, for example, has put on display a working modern sawmill. The state produces over three billion board feet of lumber per year, cut from its vast commercial forest lands. At the opposite end of the country, in Salem, Oregon, forestry and logging were recently employed as the

A model re-creating the 1969 Apollo 11 Moon Walk,
at the Southeastern Fair in Atlanta, Georgia

basic theme for the Oregon State Fair. There were elaborate
exhibits relating to forestry management and forest products,
and the entertainment features included logging events.

Many fair planners search for a different theme for each
annual fair. Sometimes these are related to an important anniversary or commemorate some special event or outstanding
individual. Some themes, at first glance, seem rather far-
fetched. The Iowa State Fair has had a Discover Mexico
theme, a Discover Canada theme, and a Discover Hawaii
theme at three consecutive fairs. The replica of a Mexican

village and the Mexican crafts, music, costumes, and food that pervaded the first of these theme fairs were a great success with both exhibitors and visitors. Similarly the Canadian fair, with its north-woods trappings, and the Hawaiian fair, with its Hawaiian village, attracted strong interest. Iowa and Hawaii, the fair management reasoned, were not really so far apart in a business sense, as Iowa produces a lot of pork and Hawaiians eat a lot of pork.

The Global Village of the State Fair of Texas and the International Shows of the State Fair of Oklahoma and of Georgia's Southeastern Fair take visitors even farther afield by means of exhibits at which they can witness a Japanese tea ceremony, buy Philippine handwork, sample Danish cheeses, or go on an African film safari.

An opportunity for Georgia fairgoers to become better acquainted with the state of Israel at Atlanta's Southeastern Fair

Viewing the work of renowned artist Ben Shahn
at a special art exhibit at the New York State Fair

While the general public has long been encouraged to submit samples of its art and photography for shows and competitions at state and county fairs, some fairs also have taken steps to exhibit the work of famous professional artists, although on a smaller scale than the fine-arts exhibits at most world's fairs. As people from rural areas and many from smaller towns and cities seldom get the opportunity to visit an art gallery or museum, a great cultural service is performed in bringing the art museum to the fair.

At the New York State Fair's Art and Home Center, there have been notable exhibits by both traditionalist and experimental figures in the world of painting, graphics, and photography. Although some of the works displayed have been jarring, producing cultural shock waves in viewers, many visitors have had their imaginations stirred and their interest aroused by these new experiences.

As the history of the United States lengthens, so does its cultural heritage. Today there is a growing awareness of the past, partly because it fills us with pride, partly because it makes us laugh at ourselves, partly because it evokes a pleasing nostalgia at a time when the future seems so baffling and uncertain. We do not know where we are going, but at least we can see where we have been.

Relics and reconstructions of our heritage charm and intrigue us at fairs and often offer a welcome retreat, away from the pressing crowds, the roar of the grandstand, the ceaseless motion of the midway. Carriage museums show us a variety

Farmhouse interior at the Daniel Parrish Witter Agricultural Museum on the New York State fairgrounds

of antique horse-drawn vehicles; railroad museums tell us about the "iron horse" steam locomotives of yesterday; and agricultural museums display the implements of old-fashioned farm life, from butter churns to blacksmith shops.

Another dip into the past is provided by events such as the Historic Automobile Exhibition, a regular feature of the New

Fascination with a 1915 Mack truck
at the New York State Fair's Historic Automobile Exhibition

Musical and photographic memorabilia
in the New York State Fair's Music Museum

York State Fair. Horseless carriages, from the steam- and
electric-powered vehicles of 1906 to classics and customized
cars of more recent vintage, are all part of the grand parade,
with prizes awarded for both the cars and the costumes of
drivers and passengers, which must be in keeping with the
car's year and model.

A collection of musical memorabilia, probably unique to
the New York State Fair, is housed in the Music Museum with
its assortment of old Edison phonographs, early jukeboxes,

Prisoners' stocks at the Danbury Fair's
New Amsterdam Village restoration

reed organs, and player pianos. This is a working museum—a
selection from its 1500 rolls of player piano music tinkles away
joyously at the command of the visitor; the nickelodeon plays
hit records of the 1920's for the traditional nickel; and an
organist is usually on hand to breathe life into one of the old
pipe organs.

And, wrapping up the past completely at fairs, there are
entire reconstructed historic villages, from amazingly authentic
New England hamlets with white-steepled churches and one-
room schoolhouses to Old West boom towns of the gold-rush
years with music halls and stagecoach rides. The New Amsterdam village at Connecticut's Danbury Fair has twenty-six
Dutch-replica buildings that evoke seventeenth-century life in
old New York and the Hudson Valley, including a courthouse,
jail, village shops, working craftsmen, and homes.

A Mohegan Indian performing the traditional "eagle dance" of his Plains brethren at the Bethlehem, Connecticut, fair

The heritage of the oldest Americans takes rightful priority at many fairs, with Indian-village reconstructions, including exhibits of crafts, costumes, agriculture, hunting and fishing implements, ceremonial dances, and other aspects of American Indian culture, generally related to the historic tribes of the region in which the fair is held.

Other ethnic backgrounds of Americans are also celebrated. A Southwestern state or county fair will have its Latin fiesta day to pay tribute to the culture of Mexican-Americans; a Southern fair may have its French, Spanish, or Creole festivity days; a Midwestern fair celebrates the Czech, German, or Scandinavian backgrounds of many of its participants and visitors. And other fairs honor the Greek, Italian, Near Eastern, Far Eastern, or other national origins of those who regularly attend them.

For fairs are, after all, people. Fairs have spanned the centuries, a mirror of the evolving human condition. They instruct us about the past, inform us about the present, and inspire us for the future. Fairs have endured simply because they offer us this image of ourselves as related to our community, our nation, and our world.

The state and county fairs, in particular, are key public-service institutions; an intimate, flexible, responsive reflection of man and his ever-changing occupations, habits, interests, achievements, needs, hopes, tastes, and desires. If we could peer into a crystal ball to see only the fairs of the future, we would probably get an amazingly accurate picture of what lies ahead for civilization on our planet.

100 Major Fairs in the USA

ALABAMA

Birmingham   Alabama State Fair
Montgomery   South Alabama State Fair

ALASKA

Palmer   Alaska State Fair

ARIZONA

Phoenix   Arizona State Fair

ARKANSAS

Little Rock   Arkansas State Fair and Livestock Show

CALIFORNIA

Sacramento   California State Fair
Pomona   Los Angeles County Fair
San Mateo   San Mateo County Fair
Stockton   San Joaquin County Fair

COLORADO

Pueblo   Colorado State Fair

CONNECTICUT

Danbury   Danbury Fair

DELAWARE
Harrington   Delaware State Fair

FLORIDA
Orlando   Central Florida Fair
Miami   Dade County Youth Fair
Tampa   Florida State Fair
Jacksonville   Greater Jacksonville Fair
West Palm Beach   South Florida Fair

GEORGIA
Columbus   Chattahoochee Valley Fair
Savannah   Coastal Empire Fair
Macon   Georgia State Fair
Atlanta   Southeastern Fair

IDAHO
Blackfoot   Eastern Idaho State Fair
Boise   Western Idaho Fair

ILLINOIS
DuQuoin   DuQuoin State Fair
Peoria   Heart of Illinois Fair
Springfield   Illinois State Fair

INDIANA
Goshen   Elkhart County 4-H Fair
Indianapolis   Indiana State Fair
Brownstown   Jackson County Fair
Crown Point   Lake County Fair

IOWA
Spencer   Clay County Fair
Davenport   Great Mississippi Valley Fair
Des Moines   Iowa State Fair

KANSAS
Hutchinson   Kansas State Fair
Topeka   Mid America Fair

KENTUCKY
Louisville   Kentucky State Fair

LOUISIANA
Shreveport   Louisiana State Fair

MAINE
Skowhegan   Skowhegan State Fair

MARYLAND
Timonium   Maryland State Fair

MASSACHUSETTS
West Springfield   Eastern States Exposition
Topsfield   Topsfield Fair

MICHIGAN
Allegan   Allegan County Fair
Ionia   Ionia Free Fair
Kalamazoo   Kalamazoo County Fair
Detroit   Michigan State Fair
Saginaw   Saginaw Fair

MINNESOTA
St. Paul   Minnesota State Fair
Austin   Mower County Fair

MISSISSIPPI
Tupelo   Mississippi Alabama Fair
Jackson   Mississippi State Fair

MISSOURI
Kansas City   American Royal Livestock Show

Sedalia	Missouri State Fair
Springfield	Ozark Empire Fair

MONTANA

Billings	Midland Empire State Fair
Great Falls	State Fair

NEBRASKA

Lincoln	Nebraska State Fair

NEVADA

Reno	Nevada State Fair

NEW HAMPSHIRE

Deerfield	Deerfield Fair
Contoocook	Hopkinton Fair

NEW JERSEY

Trenton	New Jersey State Fair

NEW MEXICO

Albuquerque	New Mexico State Fair

NEW YORK

Hamburg	Erie County Fair
Syracuse	New York State Fair

NORTH CAROLINA

Winston-Salem	Dixie Classic Fair
Charlotte	Metrolina Fair and Exposition
Raleigh	North Carolina State Fair

NORTH DAKOTA

Minot	North Dakota State Fair

OHIO

Canfield	Canfield Fair

Berea	Cuyahoga County Fair
Columbus	Ohio State Fair

OKLAHOMA

Muskogee	Muskogee State Fair
Oklahoma City	State Fair of Oklahoma
Tulsa	Tulsa State Fair

OREGON

Salem	Oregon State Fair

PENNSYLVANIA

Clearfield	Clearfield County Fair
Meadville	Crawford County Fair
Allentown	Great Allentown Fair
Reading	Reading Fair
York	York Interstate Fair

SOUTH CAROLINA

Anderson	Anderson Fair
Spartanburg	Piedmont Interstate Fair
Columbia	South Carolina State Fair

SOUTH DAKOTA

Sioux Falls	Sioux Empire Fair
Huron	South Dakota State Fair

TENNESSEE

Memphis	Mid South Fair
Nashville	Tennessee State Fair
Knoxville	Tennessee Valley Fair

TEXAS

Waco	Heart O' Texas Fair
Lubbock	Panhandle South Plains Fair

Beaumont	South Texas State Fair
Dallas	State Fair of Texas
Amarillo	Tri State Fair
Abilene	West Texas Fair

UTAH
Salt Lake City   Utah State Fair

VERMONT
Rutland   Vermont State Fair

VIRGINIA
Richmond   Virginia State Fair

WASHINGTON
Spokane   Spokane Interstate Fair

WEST VIRGINIA
Lewisburg   West Virginia State Fair

WISCONSIN
Milwaukee   Wisconsin State Fair

WYOMING
Douglas   Wyoming State Fair

Index

* indicates illustration

Lila Perl was born and educated in New York City, and she holds a B.A. degree from Brooklyn College. In addition, she has taken graduate work at Teachers College, Columbia University, and at the School of Education, New York University. She is the author of a number of books for adults and for children, both fiction and nonfiction. Several of them concern life in other lands. Her husband, Charles Yerkow, is also a writer, and they live in Beechhurst, N. Y.